Gordon is a Moron

Books by Vernon Coleman include:

The Medicine Men (1975)
Paper Doctors (1976)
Stress Control (1978)
The Home Pharmacy (1980)
Aspirin or Ambulance (1980)
Face Values (1981)
The Good Medicine Guide (1982)
Bodypower (1983)
Thomas Winsden's Cricketing Almanack (1983)
Diary of a Cricket Lover (1984)
Bodysense (1984)
Life Without Tranquillisers (1985)
The Story Of Medicine (1985, 1998)
Mindpower (1986)
Addicts and Addictions (1986)
Dr Vernon Coleman's Guide To Alternative Medicine (1988)
Stress Management Techniques (1988)
Know Yourself (1988)
The Health Scandal (1988)
The 20 Minute Health Check (1989)
Sex For Everyone (1989)
Mind Over Body (1989)
Eat Green Lose Weight (1990)
How To Overcome Toxic Stress (1990)
Why Animal Experiments Must Stop (1991)
The Drugs Myth (1992)
Complete Guide To Sex (1993)
How to Conquer Backache (1993)
How to Conquer Pain (1993)
Betrayal of Trust (1994)
Know Your Drugs (1994, 1997)
Food for Thought (1994, revised edition 2000)
The Traditional Home Doctor (1994)
People Watching (1995)
Relief from IBS (1995)
The Parent's Handbook (1995)
Men in Dresses (1996)
Power over Cancer (1996)

Crossdressing (1996)
How to Conquer Arthritis (1996)
High Blood Pressure (1996)
How To Stop Your Doctor Killing You (1996, revised edition 2003)
Fighting For Animals (1996)
Alice and Other Friends (1996)
Spiritpower (1997)
How To Publish Your Own Book (1999)
How To Relax and Overcome Stress (1999)
Animal Rights – Human Wrongs (1999)
Superbody (1999)
Complete Guide to Life (2000)
Strange But True (2000)
Daily Inspirations (2000)
Stomach Problems: Relief At Last (2001)
How To Overcome Guilt (2001)
How To Live Longer (2001)
Sex (2001)
We Love Cats (2002)
England Our England (2002)
Rogue Nation (2003)
People Push Bottles Up Peaceniks (2003)
The Cats' Own Annual (2003)
Confronting The Global Bully (2004)
Saving England (2004)
Why Everything Is Going To Get Worse Before It Gets Better (2004)
The Secret Lives of Cats (2004)
The Cat Basket (2005)
The Truth They Won't Tell You (And Don't Want You To Know) About The EU (2005)
Living in a Fascist Country (2006)
How To Protect and Preserve Your Freedom, Identity and Privacy (2006)
The Cataholic's Handbook (2006)
Animal Experiments: Simple Truths (2006)
Coleman's Laws (2006)
Secrets of Paris (2007)
Cat Fables (2007)
Too Sexy To Print (2007)
Oil Apocalypse (2007)

novels
The Village Cricket Tour (1990)
The Bilbury Chronicles (1992)
Bilbury Grange (1993)
Mrs Caldicot's Cabbage War (1993)
Bilbury Revels (1994)
Deadline (1994)
The Man Who Inherited a Golf Course (1995)
Bilbury Pie (1995)
Bilbury Country (1996)
Second Innings (1999)
Around the Wicket (2000)
It's Never Too Late (2001)
Paris In My Springtime (2002)
Mrs Caldicot's Knickerbocker Glory (2003)
Too Many Clubs And Not Enough Balls (2005)
Tunnel (1980, 2005)
Mr Henry Mulligan (2007)
Bilbury Village (2008)

as Edward Vernon
Practice Makes Perfect (1977)
Practise What You Preach (1978)
Getting Into Practice (1979)
Aphrodisiacs – An Owner's Manual (1983)

with Alice
Alice's Diary (1989)
Alice's Adventures (1992)

with Donna Antoinette Coleman
How To Conquer Health Problems Between Ages 50 and 120 (2003)
Health Secrets Doctors Share With Their Families (2005)

Gordon Is A Moron

The Definitive And Objective Analysis Of Gordon Brown's Decade As Chancellor Of The Exchequer

Vernon Coleman

Published by Blue Books, Publishing House, Trinity Place,
Barnstaple, Devon EX32 9HG, England.

This book is copyright. Enquiries should be addressed to the
author c/o the publishers.

Reprinted 2007 (twice), 2008 (seven times), 2009 (twice)

ISBN: 978-1-899726-08-0

A catalogue record for this book is available from
the British Library.

Printed by CPI Antony Rowe

Dedication

To Donna Antoinette who, like me, would have preferred another cat book, but whose kindness, wisdom, support and knowledge of when to apply a cool hand to a fevered brow, enabled me to survive the excruciating pain of writing *Gordon is a Moron*

Contents

'Gordon is a moron. Gordon is a moron.'

JILTED JOHN (FROM A 1978 HIT SONG)

Preface

In *Gordon is a Moron* I have concentrated on Gordon Brown's work as Chancellor of the Exchequer, and upon the impact his efforts have had on the economy and on our economic future.

I have not dealt in any detail with other decisions (such as the invasions of Afghanistan and Iraq) which he supported and continues to support, if those decisions did not fall directly within his remit as Chancellor of the Exchequer. Brown's failure to take a moral stand on important issues such as these merely reflects upon his moral qualities rather than on his intelligence. I have judged Brown as a Chancellor in the same way that a civil engineer might judge Hitler as a road maker.

The dictionary defines a moron as a stupid person. I don't think anyone reading this book will be left in any doubt that Gordon Brown, darling of the left wing, and widely acclaimed by the intellectually disadvantaged media proponents of fascism as a heavyweight political intellectual, is a moron; a truly stupid person.

Brown's term as Chancellor will, I believe, be remembered for poor decisions, prejudice (that would surely have resulted in serious charges if exhibited by anyone outside the Government) and Soviet quality attempts at social engineering.

In *Gordon is a Moron* I've explained how Brown's stupidity and incompetence have weakened Britain for generations to come.

If you share my horror at the lowering of quality and standards in public life you will, I suspect, also share my belief that no one exemplifies the lowering more dramatically than Gordon the Moron. I have tried to deal with Brown in an objective and academic way but I make no apologies if any of my contempt has seeped into my prose.

What have we done to deserve public servants such as Brown?

It must have been something pretty terrible.

Vernon Coleman August 2007

Chapter One

Gordon Brown: Visionary or Moron?

'No drug, nor alcohol, causes the fundamental ills of society.
If we're looking for the sources of our troubles, we shouldn't
test people for drugs; we should test them for stupidity,
ignorance, greed and (especially) love of power.'
P.J. O'ROURKE

I wish I hadn't had to write this book.

I wish everything in it was wrong; a figment of my imagination.

I wish we could trust the professional politicians and let them get on with running the country for us, so that we, in turn, could be allowed to get on with our lives.

Sadly, I will show in this book precisely how Gordon Brown has destroyed Britain in general (and England in particular).

No Briton in history – not even Tony Blair – has ever done as much damage to his country as Gordon Brown.

There's a myth that Gordon Brown was a great Chancellor of the Exchequer. He wasn't. Gordon Brown wasn't just sulky and grumpy. He was the worst Chancellor Britain has ever had. He was incompetent and, in my view, unfair in his treatment of the English. It seems to me that we can praise him as successful only if his aim was to destroy everything good about Britain.

While he was Chancellor of the Exchequer, Brown spent our money as if it was his own. He used it not to provide us with an infrastructure and services (that is, after all, why we hired him and trusted him with our taxes) but to prosecute political aims and social engineering programmes that would have fitted very well into the old Soviet Union.

As Chancellor, Brown was a man with a barely hidden agenda – pursuing his political ideals with money diverted from its proper purpose.

Gordon is one of life's prefects; the swot who was never as bright as he wanted to be; the Scot with a chip on his shoulder the size of a 300-year-old oak; a man seemingly inspired not by passion or generosity but by vanity and resentment.

Gordon Brown isn't just the worst Chancellor Britain has ever had; he has destroyed the British economy for years to come and has changed the nation's social structure. In ten long years, he has done enormous economic damage to the hopes and prosperity of every honest, hard-working Briton.

Day after day for the last decade there has been evidence of an interfering, manipulative and dishonest Government. Deception has been the only constancy.

Gordon Brown and his Labour Party colleagues have massaged figures, changed economic cycles, redefined basic terms such as public borrowing, announced and re-announced spending in order to convince the public they were spending more than they were on worthwhile projects, and concealed taxes. We've been betrayed by a Government of institutionally racist Bushlovers, supported by a compliant state-controlled broadcaster and an electoral system that doesn't even nod in the direction of genuine democracy.

Brown may be lionised by statist organisations such as the BBC but I believe his efforts have done more harm to Britain and the British (and, in particular, to the English) than all the overseas enemies Britain has had for half a century.

Brown is a philanthropist using other people's money to satisfy his dreams; a man who prefers Scotland to England; a man who seems to prefer superstores to village shops; a man not quite as smarmy as his predecessor but every bit as sneaky and vain; an enemy of democracy, freedom and trust; a lover of state control, means-testing and political targets; a man prepared to see countless thousands die rather than risk losing his own chauffeur-driven car.

Gordon Brown is a man who, if he painted, would paint by numbers. And everything would be shades of grey.

With Brown there is no real sense of preparation; no strategic thinking. There is, instead, just a lurching from crisis to crisis. Abraham Lincoln, 16th President of the United States of America, once said: 'If I had eight hours to chop down a tree, I'd spend seven of them sharpening my axe.' If Brown had eight hours to chop down a tree he would, I suspect, spend the first seven hours ringing up friendly editors at the BBC to arrange sympathetic photographic coverage.

By legislation, edicts, directives, council tax capping and other manifestations of Stalinism, this control freak, a man who seems to me to loathe individuality and democracy in equal amounts, has ruined our nation.

★ ★ ★

In politics the oily dross rises to the top like scum on a stagnant pond. Prescott, Blunkett, Mandelson et al earned reputations as weak, stupid or vain men. They don't have the intelligence to be truly evil. But they have the qualities to be bad men.

Brown, like his brothers in political grime, seemed to me to be constantly reaching out in a desperate attempt to touch the hem of mediocrity and failing even to get that far, stretching every sinew as he grappled with simple competence; always failing.

There is much to dislike about New Labour. The bleating, self-pitying whining from Blunkett, the almost unintelligible but clearly truculent bullying bluster of Prescott, the slimy, pustulant Mandelson (the man actually looks clammy and untrustworthy), the vanity and transparent dishonesty of Blair. The deceit of the other players. The arrogance of the courtiers.

But, while the other players strutted and preened, it was Brown who did the damage.

Brown helped encourage mass immigration (thereby exacerbating the housing crisis) and as Chancellor enjoyed the benefits of an inheritance tax scheme which meant that countless thousands had to sell their family homes to pay the punitive taxes on already taxed money. In Brown's world the elderly who need long-term care (or are bullied into it by the local Gestapo) must sell their home to pay for it. (Though, if they are lucky enough to live in Scotland, they get their long-term care entirely free of charge – paid for by English taxpayers.)

Gordon Brown is an arrogant statist, committed to the belief that all problems are best solved by central government. In addition to being pig-headed, pompous and arrogant Brown seems rude and graceless. He believes he knows better than we do how our money should be spent. Brown spends our money on projects he thinks are good for us. It's very easy to be generous with other people's money.

Brown doesn't approve of allowing people to spend their money the way they want to spend it. He believes that he knows best. Do you want to give financial support to Scottish students or would you rather mend your roof? Do you want to buy bombs to drop on Afghan wedding parties or would you rather spend your money on sending food to Africa? Don't worry your pretty little head trying to decide: Gordon will make the decision for you.

★ ★ ★

Despite attempts to keep quiet about the wars on Afghanistan and Iraq, Gordon Brown was a supporter of both and must, therefore, share responsibility for the deaths of countless thousands of innocent children in those countries. When Tony Blair eventually appears before a War Crimes Tribunal (as many people hope and believe he will) Gordon Brown will, I hope, be forced to stand alongside him.

According to David Blunkett, Brown only gave his unequivocal support to the invasion of Iraq when he realised that his own job and pension were on the line and that if he didn't support the invasion he would lose his job as Chancellor of the Exchequer. In his self-serving (and, it has to be said, largely unreadable) diaries Blunkett described how Brown decided to toe the line after a cabinet meeting on March 13th 2003, five days before the House of Commons voted for the war. Blunkett claims that Brown realised that Blair would fire him if he didn't vote for the war. And so, eschewing courage and principle in favour of statist pragmatism,

Brown dutifully voted for the war, putting his chauffeur-driven limousine above the lives of British soldiers, and his own ambition and sense of survival above whatever shreds of integrity he might have had when he had entered politics.

Gordon Brown is reported to have said that he didn't think Blunkett had ever made such an allegation and that if he was reported as having done so, he was being misquoted. But Blunkett's diary entries were published for public consumption. And they were recorded shortly after the relevant Cabinet meeting.

★ ★ ★

Do you remember the world before Brown became Chancellor of the Exchequer? A world in which dentists were available on the NHS; a world in which you could telephone your GP at night, at the weekend or on Christmas Day and speak either to him or one of his partners; a world in which people did not need to fly to Poland to have their teeth done or to India to have hip surgery; a world in which you put out your dustbin once a week and expect the council to empty it (and if you had an old fridge or bed you didn't want they'd collect that free too); a world in which policemen patrolled our streets and made them safe enough for law abiding citizens to pop out of doors after five o'clock at night. Do you still remember that old, almost forgotten world?

Blair, Prescott, Blunkett and the other dummies must take some of the responsibility for the mess that Labour has made of the country in the last decade.

But Blair was too busy starting wars and sucking up to the Americans to spend much time worrying about domestic affairs. He visited the House of Commons so rarely he probably had to ring up and get directions whenever he did bother to make an appearance. And Prescott and Blunkett were probably too busy getting their legs over to worry about boring things like rubbish collections and dentists.

The rumour that won't go away says that Gordon agreed to stand aside in the leadership contest which followed John Smith's untimely demise for two things. First, that Tony would hand over the top job during his second term and, second, for control of the domestic agenda (allowing him to bugger up Britain while leaving

Tony free to bomb other bits of the world). And thus it was that Blair managed foreign policy, started the wars and sought photo opportunities in scenic foreign cities while Brown ran domestic affairs.

And, after ten years of effectively running the country, Brown has damaged and weakened Britain to the point where countless thousands now believe that the only way forward is to emigrate. Gordon isn't just a harmless moron. I believe that he is a vain, vindictive and dangerous moron. And, in this book, I will show you precisely why I believe this to be true.

★ ★ ★

Newspaper commentators widely hailed Gordon Brown as a wise and prudent Chancellor of the Exchequer. Sadly, the evidence does not justify this praise.

Brown, the poor man's Mussolini, and now leader of Britain's unelected Government, was notoriously imprudent with other people's money. He has mortally wounded the British economy.

British industry, British investors and the vast majority of British voters all breathed a sigh of relief when Tony Blair quit number ten to make his fortune. But I believe that the woefully incompetent and indifferent Brown, a disaster as a Chancellor, will prove to be just as much a disaster as a Prime Minister. It is frightening to realise that the time might well come when British voters wish Tony Blair was back in number ten.

It is worth remembering that Lord Turnbull, Brown's former Permanent Secretary, described Brown as operating with 'Stalinist ruthlessness'. Brown's years as Chancellor were marked by spin and obfuscation. He will be remembered for his introduction of stealth taxes and for making tax legislation even more horrendously complicated than it was before. His only achievement is surely to have deceived and obfuscated so successfully that he has temporarily sustained the myth of prudence. Brown has been as effective at spin as was his dear and devoted friend Tony Blair. With Brown running the Exchequer, democracy was replaced by a complex system of deals, favours, betrayal and bribery.

★ ★ ★

How then can Gordon Brown claim that the British economy is doing well as a result of his endeavours?

Well there is, you might not be surprised to hear, a trick to this.

Three tricks actually.

The first trick is that our apparent wealth is built on our house prices. People in Britain feel and look rich because their houses have soared in value. And banks have been enthusiastically lending money to house owners who have used their homes as collateral. When the value of your house has gone up by another £100,000 the bank will happily lend you another £75,000. And what's the worry? The house will go up by another £100,000 next year or the year after.

Won't it?

It is the money borrowed against rising house prices (not money earned by making widgets) that people have been spending on new cars and new toys.

The second trick is that the economy has been kept bubbling because the Government has spent massive amounts of money on hiring thousands and thousands of new administrators and bureaucrats and building smart new offices to put them in. None of these very well-paid people do anything productive, of course. They don't bring money into the country or make widgets which can be sold. They don't design new widgets or work out new ways to use old widgets. The Government's millions of employees get paid to design and circulate red tape. And that, of course, has been slowly but very effectively destroying what is left of our manufacturing industry and the most productive parts of our service industry.

The vast number of new Government employees hired on Brown's watch seem to add to the success of the economy because they have money to spend on houses and television sets. But the money they earn and spend isn't 'real' money. It isn't money that has been brought into the country from outside. It's more like pocket money paid to the kids. When children get pocket money to spend, the local sweet shop may prosper but your household income hasn't risen.

And the third trick is a total absence of any sense of shame.

Gordon, like most of his political contemporaries, doesn't feel ashamed because he does not have a vision of reality which matches yours and mine. Like Tony Blair, his predecessor and moral inspiration, Gordon Brown lives in a Lewis Carroll world of his own where good is what he says is good and bad is always something other people do. The Government rules by force and compromise. The lobbyists and the spin-doctors have more authority than the electors. We now live in a world where, for example, the inflation figures the Government give us bear almost no resemblance to reality.

Gordon Brown and the Labour Government have created an economy which is designed to fall apart. If they had deliberately set out to destroy the country they could not have made a better job of things.

Thanks to Brown's policies, the UK will suffer more than almost any other nation in the world when oil prices start to rise as the oil runs out.

Brown constantly whines about being prudent. He is, in the words of one commentator, 'about as prudent as Imelda Marcos in a shoe shop'.

Gordon Brown has turned the pound into a very dangerous beast.

When he finally retired as Chancellor, Brown left Britain with a historic real estate bubble, a surging trade gap and a huge Government deficit. Money supply in Britain has been growing at an absurd rate. The Tories were bad enough, but Labour has finally shown us the extent to which politicians will go, and just how dangerous they can be.

In the rest of this book I will examine every aspect of Gordon Brown's ten years as Chancellor and explain precisely why he deserves the label 'moron' rather than 'political visionary'.

Chapter Two

Fiddling the Inflation Figures

'Last year, if you didn't eat, didn't drive to work, didn't heat your home, didn't visit a doctor, didn't buy a house, didn't buy insurance of any kind, didn't have a child in college and didn't pay...taxes, your cost of living agrees with the Government's cost of living index.'
CLYDE HARRISON

Whenever he stood up in the House of Commons to talk about inflation, Chancellor Brown talked blithely about the level of inflation being two to three per cent.

But in reality, this was spin.

Throughout Brown's tenure as Chancellor the real level of inflation has been far, far higher.

Between 2003 and 2006, for example, the cost of essentials rose as follows in Britain: gas by 64%, electricity by 45%, council tax by 16%, water by 24%, petrol by 28% and mortgage interest payments by 50%. House prices rose by heaven knows what. However, none of these price rises were counted by the Government when it measured inflation because none of these items are regarded as 'essential'.

Without such non-essentials as fuel and housing costs cluttering up the inflation figures, Brown was able to point, with enormous Scottish pride, to an official inflation figure of around about two per cent.

Brown forced the Bank of England to adopt a phoney price index target as the building block for its inflation figures. As a result, the Bank of England's inflation figure is entirely spurious. Fraudulent, even. The whole British economy is built upon inflation figures. By creating false inflation figures the Government is doing long-term damage to Britain.

Here's how Brown did it.

One of Brown's first actions was to give the Bank of England its 'independence' and to allow the Monetary Police Committee (MPC) to set interest rates. For this he was widely praised. But there was small print (as there always has been with Brown). The MPC had to set interest rates so as to keep inflation within a narrow band. Nothing wrong with that, of course. Except that Brown has constantly fiddled with the way that inflation is measured so that in practice it is effectively he, and not the Monetary Police Committee, which decides what interest rates will be.

When Labour arrived in office inflation was measured using the Retail Price Index. It had been thus for half a century.

Brown arbitrarily switched the way inflation is measured in Britain. He needed to do this because Government spending always stimulates the economy and he always planned to be a prince when it came to spending other people's money.

Brown got rid of the Retail Price Index (which he decided he didn't like because it tended to produce realistic inflation figures) and replaced it with the Consumer Price Index (which he decided he liked because it produces lower inflation figures). In addition, the Office of National Statistics has been bullied into using all sorts of tricks designed to 'lower' the rate of inflation and, therefore, to keep interest rates lower than they should be. (There are, of course, huge political advantages to be gained by keeping interest rates artificially low.)

One trick used to keep the official inflation figures down has been to use 'hedonics'. This is really rather crafty and typically Brown. If a product (such as a computer) can be said to be of better quality (insofar as it has, say, a bigger memory) then any rise in price can be officially recorded as a fall in price because the consumer is getting more for his money. The computer may have cost you more than the computer you bought last year but as far as Brown's inflation figures are concerned it cost you less.

Another trick is to substitute a lower priced item if one item on the list used to create inflation figures goes up too much. So, for example, if the price of beef goes up this will be ignored because the Government will assume that housewives won't buy beef but will buy chicken instead.

And the best trick of all is simply to omit from the list of items being measured anything which might go up too much and, therefore, have too great an influence on the official inflation rate.

So, for example, Brown's official inflation index omits 'non-essentials' such as food, housing and energy prices (all of which are, of course, rocketing). Even the prices of alcohol and tobacco are excluded because they tend to go up quite often. The cost of housing is also omitted since that too is now considered 'non-essential'. So, when you hear that inflation is running at two per cent, but it seems to you that the prices you pay are rising considerably faster than that, it is the Government which is wrong and not your perceptions.

Taxes too (the main expenditure for most of us) aren't included either. All this enables the Government to claim (utterly dishonestly) that it has kept inflation low. And this, in turn, enables it to cheat pensioners and others out of their real 'inflation-proofed' pay rises.

(Maybe food and energy costs are excluded from the Consumer Price Index because Brown has for a decade spent most of his time in buildings heated by taxpayers or, being driven around in cars fuelled by taxpayers.)

It is hardly surprising, in view of all this, that a group of MPs and people campaigning for pensioners estimated that the real rate of inflation was nine per cent – four times the official rate at the time.

As I've already said, it's very convenient to lie about inflation. If inflation is high then people will want big wage rises and pensioners (and others on inflation-linked incomes) have to be paid more. Naturally, pensions which are inflation-linked are increased annually according to the Government's own official figure rather than the real figure.

By divorcing the official inflation figures from reality, Brown managed to fiddle the figures and con the electorate. His craftiness has done much to harm savers, pensioners, investors and the economy. His trickery has also enabled him to claim that he has managed the economy well.

★ ★ ★

In 2007, the true inflation figure was so high that anyone receiving less than 8-10% on their investments (almost impossible to achieve without taking big risks) was losing money. Their savings were decreasing in value each year. Those who wanted their savings to grow needed a return in excess of 8-10%. There are no safe ways to do this and so the Government was putting savers in a position where they either had to accept that their money was decreasing in purchasing power or they had to take great risks with their savings. It is hardly surprising that saving levels have reached abysmally low levels. What is the point in saving money when it is clear to anyone not in the Government, or working for compliant sectors of the media, that the pound you earn today will buy you more if you spend it now than it will if you put it aside for a rainy day?

The enduring problem with all this is the fact that as people realise that the money they work for and save and hold in their bank accounts (or in a sock under the bed) is becoming worthless so they want to get rid of it and exchange it for something more enduring. Anything. Art. Flat screen television sets. Houses. No one trusts the Government any more. And no one trusts the currency either.

★ ★ ★

Most people alive have never seen real inflation at first hand. But it can be truly scary.

Look at what happened in 1923 in Germany.

As a schoolboy I was enormously impressed to have stamps in my album that were worth 500 million marks. Five hundred million marks to post a letter. Stamps had to be overprinted with new values by the local postmaster because by the time they got from the printer to the post offices their values were laughably inadequate.

28

None of this is exceptional. It happens all the time. In April 2007, the Zimbabwean dollar was pegged to the American version at the rate of 15,000 to one. By June, just two months later, the rate was 200,000 to one. Useful to tourists no doubt. But not much fun if your wealth is tied up in Zimbabwean dollars. By July 2007, inflation in Zimbabwe was said to be 5,000% and prices were going up by 10% a day. People going to the bank were limited to withdrawing one and a half million Zimbabwean dollars from the bank at a time. This may sound like a lot of money but it meant queuing at the bank for four consecutive days to draw out enough money to buy a tankful of petrol.

It is happening in Britain too. Not as quickly, perhaps. But it is happening. In 2007, a pound was worth about a tenth of what it had been worth just thirty years earlier.

Chapter Three
The Great Pensions Theft

'Anyone can get old. All you have to do is live long enough.'
GROUCHO MARX

Whatever else he does with his life Gordon the Moron will always be remembered for one thing: he deliberately, wilfully stole the pensions of millions, and single-handedly destroyed both the principle of saving and the lives of millions of the hardest working men and women in Britain. It was a cruel and ruthless act which has caused enormous hardship.

Brown's single, most ruthless and damaging act was to alter the rules governing the way pensions are taxed. Doing this enabled him to take countless billions out of the pensions of hard working men and women.

The money gouged out of pension funds was used to enable the Labour Government to hire nearly a million additional public sector workers. The majority of these new employees have purposeless administrative posts but most of them will vote Labour in gratitude for the work, salaries and perks they have been given.

The damage done to the pensions of people working outside the public sector is almost incalculable and unimaginable. The pensions snatch was an act of premeditated malice.

Brown was warned by officials about the damaging consequences of grabbing money from pension funds. It has been reported that other Ministers in the Cabinet 'didn't have a clue' what was happening. The pension snatch was, it seems certain, Brown's work alone. The consequences have been disastrous for pensioners, the stock market and those on low incomes. Brown's pension grab is the reason why millions of pensioners, people who worked and saved hard all their lives, will spend their final years in penury; shivering in the cold. It is because of Brown's policies that many younger Britons no longer contribute to pension schemes.

The moment I heard what he had done I warned (in 1997) that Brown had created a massive and enduring problem for British pensioners. Sadly, this has proved to be the case. It is estimated that Brown's tax changes took £150 billion out of pension funds, destroying the hopes and futures of British pensioners.

Why didn't politicians in the other parties see the danger in Brown's pension snatch? I'm no expert on pensions but at the time it seemed clear that Brown's actions would do huge damage to the retirement years of millions of hard working pensioners.

When it was pointed out that Brown had been warned in 1997 that his tax grab would cost pensioners around £150 billion, and cause a huge shortfall in pension funds, Brown's spin-doctors argued that the snatch and grab was arranged on the advice of civil servants. (This is standard Labour Party policy: if you are in a tight corner, blame unknown civil servants who aren't allowed to speak up for themselves and who know that as long as they keep quiet they won't be identified, lose their jobs or be disciplined.)

Brown also damaged pension funds by introducing new accounting rules that forced fund managers to provide a snapshot valuation of the market value of their assets and liabilities. This did enormous damage by effectively forcing insurance companies and pension funds to take a large amount of their money out of equities and to put it into Government bonds. Naturally, this proved extremely convenient for Brown since it enabled the Government to issue a constant stream of bonds and to create yet more Government debt.

(Brown has issued vast quantities of Government bonds or gilts to finance welfare expenditure and to pay for hiring more civil servants. Every year interest has to be paid on the bonds which have been issued. And eventually the capital will have to be repaid to those who invested in the bonds. Brown has lumbered future generations with a huge bill.)

Over the years equities have always proved to be a far better investment but Brown wanted pension fund money invested in Government bonds instead.

Brown's instruction to the Pensions Regulator ensured that the Government had little difficulty in raising vast amounts of debt but it has also ensured that pension funds have done even worse than they might otherwise have expected.

Gordon Brown has destroyed pensions for people who have productive jobs. He has destroyed pensions for the rapidly diminishing few, the few who do all the work, take the risks and keep the nation from the bailiffs.

When confronted with this awful truth, a truth from which any sensitive, caring human being would shrink, Brown effectively said: 'Yes I did it and I am proud of what I did and what I did.'

In addition to grabbing money out of pension funds, Brown also introduced new rules allegedly designed to 'simplify' pensions.

However, the 'simplification' of pensions has made the whole subject utterly incomprehensible – even for many professionals. Brown never misses an opportunity to make something simple more complicated than it is or needs to be.

Brown's most recent changes to pensions legislation resulted in the introduction of more than 600 pages of legislation (nearly double what was there before) and another 1,500 pages of technical guidance (a fourfold increase on what was envisaged in 2004). In the *Financial Times*, John Lawson, the head of pensions policy at Standard Life Assurance, was quoted as saying that: 'very few advisers have got to grips with the implications of the protection available on accrued pension rights'. He described the legislation and the guidance as 'impenetrable'. If the experts find the legislation 'impenetrable' it seems likely that ordinary workers might also find it difficult to understand. This, of course, will suit the Government. When people don't understand the rules they tend to make mistakes. And when they make mistakes they can be disciplined and, more importantly, fined.

Brown's pension simplification has made life impossible for would-be savers. Taking out a £100,000 loan or mortgage (that can hardly be afforded) requires less paperwork than putting £20 into one of the Government's stakeholder pensions. It is, perhaps, not surprising that new pension schemes have proved remarkably unpopular and have attracted very little interest from those who most need to be saving for their old age.

The destructive tax grab which destroyed pensions and life for millions of pensioners will not affect the massive inflation-proof index-linked pensions paid to civil servants, MPs and former Ministers. These pensions are paid for by taxpayers.

Brown's pension grab ensured that Britain will, in future, be divided in two: those receiving their pensions directly from the Government (as a result of some form of Government employment) and those receiving private pensions. Those in the first group will be the new rich. Those in the second group will, on the whole, be the new poor.

Public sector workers can retire at the age of 60 at the latest. They receive final salary-linked pensions for which taxpayers are responsible. Yet, thanks to Brown, people outside the state sector will soon not be able to claim a state pension until they reach 68 years of age, and even then it will not be enough to live on.

Outside central Government, the cost of providing pensions for town hall staff is rocketing. By mid 2007, a quarter of the average council tax bill was being spent paying for the solid gold pensions of town hall staff. And the cost was forecast to rise by another 17% by 2008. The cost of the local Government pension scheme has trebled since Gordon Brown was made Chancellor of the Exchequer.

Since Government pension schemes are all Ponzi schemes the taxes collected in, say, 2008, are used only to pay the pensions paid in 2008 to people who have already retired. (A Ponzi scheme – named after the fraudster Charles Ponzi – is a form of fraud in which the first investors get paid with money provided by later investors. This is not just similar to the pension scheme run by the Government – it is exactly the same as the scheme run by the Government. And it's a scheme that is illegal if organised by anyone else.)

The future pensions of current workers will have to be paid by future taxpayers. As more and more council workers retire, so the public sector pensions bill will continue to soar.

Ponzi schemes are illegal because they are pyramid selling schemes. A few people always do well out of them. But most people lose. If the State was a private company Brown would have been arrested for fraud a long time ago.

There are still some people around who pay tax and National Insurance and assume that the State is putting aside some of their contributions to pay for their pension when it becomes due. But that's not how things happen. Taxes and National Insurance contributions are used to pay pensions to *today's* pensioners.

I'll put that another way: the pensions of today's workers will be paid by tomorrow's workers – if they can afford it. The State recklessly assumes that the amount of tax paid by tomorrow's workers will be enough to pay the pensions of today's workers.

Remember, we are not simply talking here about State pensions (a big enough liability) but about the massive, final salary, inflation-proofed pensions paid to State employees.

The State assumes that the economy will grow for ever. And that in five, ten and twenty years time tax receipts will be sufficient to pay all its pension obligations.

This is, as I've already said, a fraudulent scheme which would result in long terms of imprisonment for those running it if it were a private enterprise.

Everything goes well as long as the economy continues to grow and tax receipts continue to rise.

But the economy isn't going to continue to grow. And tax receipts won't continue to rise.

★ ★ ★

The Government's Financial assistance Scheme, set up to help people whose company pensions have collapsed (quite probably as a result of Brown's pension grab) cost £7 million to run in the first 18 months of its existence. But it paid out only £3 million during that time. Just 871 people out of 125,000 whose company pension had collapsed received any money.

★ ★ ★

The unfunded cost of public sector pensions has now reached at least £720 billion. There is an additional £90 billion owing on local government pensions. (These are conservative figures, as estimated by the Centre for Policy Studies. The total figure, according to other experts, could be as high as £1,025 billion.) Much of the money paid by taxpayers is now used to service public service pensions.

Brown has created a system of apartheid in Britain.

On the one side there are the public service workers who can retire young on huge pensions. On the other side are those on private pensions who must work on into their late sixties and seventies and, even then, retire on inadequate pensions.

Private sector workers have suffered twice under Brown. Their own pensions have been destroyed and yet they are expected to pay for the gold plated pensions of public sector workers.

It used to be argued that public sector workers needed to receive better pensions because they earned smaller salaries. This may have been true before Brown. But it is not true now. The average public sector worker receives nearly 15% more pay than the average private sector worker. (And has much better holidays, sick pay entitlement and perks.)

You will doubtless be relieved to hear that Brown's own pension is safe. He will probably receive at least £117,500 a year plus £90,000 a year to pay for secretarial staff (staff who will doubtless be needed to co-ordinate the writing of his autobiography and the arranging of his extremely profitable lecture tours).

Having destroyed the pension of anyone who doesn't work for the Government, Gordon can look forward to an index-linked pension paid by the beleaguered British taxpayer. Brown's pension would require a pension pot of over £3 million. However, anyone who was rich enough to build up a pension pot that big would be stupid to do so because Brown introduced a special tax rate of 55% on any pension fund which exceeds £1.5 million. This cap doesn't apply to Ministers or senior Government employees.

Why does the phrase 'one law for us and one law for him' spring to mind?

MPs can hardly complain about Brown's self preservation for they too have it made. MPs have voted themselves millions of pounds of taxpayers' money to top up their pension shortfall. The pensions of the civil servants who helped Brown destroy pension funds are safe too for the time being.

Who will pay all those pension obligations in a few years time when the economy has slumped and the Government's income has collapsed? (Both of which will happen.)

No one.

Countless millions who are expecting to be able to live on their State pensions (and millions of central and local government employees who are expecting to receive a generous final salary scheme) have a terrible shock coming.

When the oil has run out and the economy stops growing there simply will not be anywhere near enough money available to pay all those pension obligations.

Nor, of course, will there be any money available to pay unemployment or sickness benefits. And millions of people who thought that they had secure jobs with the Government will suddenly find that their jobs aren't quite so secure after all.

Vernon Coleman

Chapter Four

How Brown's Performance Target Culture Has Destroyed Public Services

'Freedom does not die in one blow, it dies
by inches in public legislation.'
LORD STRATHCLYDE,

Brown is a believer in performance targets and it his fault that public services have been afflicted by an absurd and dangerous 'target culture'.

Naively, and rather stupidly, Brown seems to believe that if you give public servants targets they will work harder and provide a better service. Indeed, like any good Soviet dictator, Brown seems to believe that he only had to announce a target for it to become an achievement.

Brown set spending review targets (known as public service agreements or PSAs) which covered the performance of all the major Government departments and which set highly complex and specific criteria for the way in which public servants are assessed. The PSAs cover everything from exam results to crime figures and cancer rates.

What Brown didn't realise (possibly because of a lack of much genuine work experience – he's been an MP since the age of 32) is that when you give public servants targets they will concentrate on satisfying those targets to the exclusion of everything else. Self-preservation takes over, the target becomes the aim and the focus, and the welfare and indeed the existence of the public, the individual, the person, the end user, the patient, the client, the poor taxpayer hoping to get some service for their money, goes out of the window, never to be seen again. The end result is a massive fraud. Public servants are encouraged to cheat the public in order to get promoted and to receive bonus payments.

Performance indicators on a scale that would have impressed Stalin have been forced on councils, schools, hospitals, the police and institutions throughout the nation. Gordon the Moron has helped create a crazy world in which every public employee is more concerned with meeting 'targets' than in satisfying the public's needs.

It was Brown who created the entirely mad world in which public services can claim that they are providing the public with wonderful service even though everyone with half a brain knows that they are not.

Gordon Brown's endless series of targets gave him control over other Government Departments and the way they worked. If doctors or policemen didn't do things the way he said they should then they wouldn't get the money they needed to do their jobs. By controlling the purse strings at the Treasury, and making other departments obey his targets, Brown interfered in a way never seen before in Britain.

Brownism meant that a bunch of people who knew nothing about vital services such as health, education and crime fighting were effectively in control of health, education and crime fighting. Incompetent professionals were able to behave ever more incompetently. Unimaginative, uncaring jobsworth bureaucrats who worked by the rulebook were able to rise through the ranks and take control. For them Brown's targets were a dream come true. Politically-correct nurses, policemen and teachers now all had excuses for ignoring the needs of their patients, citizens and pupils. Millions of public servants who were being paid to serve the public now had just one master: Gordon. Instead of pleasing the public all they had to do was meet their targets and success and glory would be theirs. It is to their eternal shame that so many professionals should submit so meekly to such nonsense.

Some of the targets introduced were nothing short of mad. So, for example, the Atomic Energy Authority was told that it must increase its favourable media coverage by 43.9%. Kew Gardens was told that it must receive 30,000 herbarium specimens a year.

Hospitals were told that patients who visited casualty departments had to be seen within four hours. (I confess that I have always found this woefully unambitious. Can you imagine Gordon Brown sitting in a casualty department waiting four hours to have one of his family seen by a nurse? No, nor can I.)

Hospitals got round these woefully unambitious casualty waiting time targets by employing a 'hello' nurse. The nurse just says 'hello' but doesn't offer any treatment. But she is officially the end of the waiting time.

Struggle into a Brownian casualty department with a leg hanging off and a nurse will totter over and say 'Hello'. That's it. 'Hello'. But officially you've been seen within four hours. It is deceitful and dishonest and so it fits the Labour Government's style like a rubber glove.

In other hospitals the result of Brownian targets is that patients wait for seven hours because they are placed in 'medical assessment units' where, although they still haven't been treated, they don't officially count as still waiting.

Before April 2004, GPs provided out of hours patient care, including weekends and bank holidays. But then the Labour Government offered GPs a new contract which entitled them to opt out of providing 24 hour a day 365 days a year cover for their patients. (It was this new contract which also enabled GPs to dramatically increase their incomes well into six figures. The Government, under Gordon Brown's financial guidance, negotiated a deal which, by 2007, gave GPs an average income of £118,000 – an increase of 63% on what they were earning when they had to work nights and weekends.) The overall result of the change was that the cost of providing out of hours care doubled and the quality of care provided for patients slumped dramatically.

> A mother died despite being seen by eight doctors in four days. The woman's own local surgery had closed for Easter and the doctors she saw were providing an out of hours service. As a result she spoke to a different doctor every time she telephoned. And, of course, the doctors had no access to her medical records (locked up in her GP's surgery) or to the notes made by the other emergency doctors to whom she had spoken. Since 1997, the number of nurses in the NHS has gone up by 17% and the number of bureaucrats has increased by 45%.

NHS administrators are now telling English patients that if they want to jump a queue or take a forbidden drug by paying for it privately they will not be allowed to have any free NHS medical care (even though they will, if they are British citizens, have paid for such care through their taxes and National Insurance contributions). So, for example, bureaucrats are now arguing (and this, I believe, is a new policy introduced under Gordon Brown's control of the purse strings) that a patient who is refused a drug for the treatment of his illness and opts to try to stay alive by selling his home and buying the drug, must also pay for any other treatment he requires (such as X-rays, scans and surgery etc..). This is not only grotesquely unfair, it is also intensely hypocritical since NHS hospitals, and staff working full-time for the NHS, are now allowed and even encouraged to use NHS facilities to earn extra money by offering private services. Moreover, the staff are allowed to do this in time which should be used for caring for NHS patients. The NHS is, therefore, deliberately creating a shortage of NHS facilities so that it can sell those same facilities to patients who might otherwise die while waiting for investigations or treatment to be provided under the NHS. Patients in Scotland, Gordon Brown's home country, are not abused in this way and do not need to sell their homes to try to stay alive.

The NHS as financed by Gordon Brown spends £1.5 billion a year on management consultants but cannot afford £2.50 a day for drugs needed by English patients with Alzheimer's disease. The drugs which English patients are denied can delay the progress of symptoms such as memory loss and personality changes. (Patients living in Gordon Brown's home country of Scotland get all the drugs they need. Gordon Brown would receive drugs for Alzheimer's Disease if he needed them because he is Scottish.)

The organisation which banned the drugs is called NICE (the National Institute for Health and Clinical Excellence). NICE was set up by the Labour Government in 1999 to decide which medication and treatments should not be made available to patients in England and Wales.

> A council's care provider assessment expert decided that helping a 99-year-old woman up and down stairs was too dangerous for council staff. The council said they were worried that the 4 foot 9 inch tall seven stone woman might fall on the helpers and injure them.

The elderly are now treated as irrelevant and disposable in the British NHS. I frequently receive mail from readers telling me that they have noticed that as they (or their relatives) reach certain age milestones (seventy is the one most commonly quoted) medical care is withdrawn. Patients who are considered 'too old' are quite likely to be denied investigations and treatment. It doesn't matter how fit they are – they will be left to die simply because of their biological age. Age discrimination has been officially authorised by the Government which has effectively institutionalised ageism. In mid August 2007, a Select Committee on Human Rights, consisting of MPs and peers, reported that 21% of hospitals and care homes fail to meet even minimum standards of dignity and privacy for older people. The Committee said it had uncovered evidence of neglect, abuse, discrimination and unfair treatment of frail, older people. (Their discovery came as no surprise to those of us who have been uncovering such abuse for decades.)

In one afternoon in September 2006, an English coroner heard how incompetence and neglect may have contributed to the deaths of three elderly men and one elderly woman. A 75-year-old man was left to starve on a hospital ward. A war veteran was left to lie in his own excrement.

In the modern NHS, the most vulnerable patients are the ones who are being abandoned and being denied the most basic care. I have a file of reports detailing instances in which patients have been treated with unbelievable callousness by nurses and administrators. And, indeed, I have witnessed this sort of reprehensible behaviour at first hand. It sounds absurd but I have stood in a British teaching hospital and watched in horror as nurses ignored pleas from patients who needed bedpans or were unable to feed themselves. I have seen patients forced to lie, hungry, and stare at food which had been cruelly and tantalisingly placed in front of them but which they could not eat without help – help which never came. The number of patients leaving NHS hospitals suffering from malnourishment rose by two thirds in the last half of Gordon Brown's Chancellorship. In 2006, an astonishing 2,265 people left hospital lacking basic nourishment. In 2001, the figure was 1,381. In some areas of Britain nearly half of hospital patients report that they don't get enough help with eating.

And, while patients lay starving, a total of 13 million hospital meals were thrown away untouched. Between 2001 and 2006 hospital food costing £162 million was thrown away – not just because it was inedible (which much of it was) but because patients were too ill to eat it without help and no one was prepared to help feed them.

> A recent survey from Help the Aged shows that 144,000 old people never leave their homes. This is sometimes because they are too frightened to go out. It is often because they can't afford to go out. Over a fifth of pensioners now live in poverty.

GPs are now paid according to whether or not they 'hit' their targets. So, for example, GPs search over-assiduously for hidden ailments and now frequently label patients as having disorders they do not have, and coerce them into taking drugs they do not need, in order to hit their own targets and to earn more money. Today's GPs no longer have a direct responsibility to their patients but, too often, regard their patients as a means to an end – the end being the number of patients they can diagnose as being diabetic, treat with blood pressure lowering drugs or treat with cholesterol lowering drugs. Brown's accursed targets have destroyed what was left of the traditional doctor-patient relationship.

In some parts of the country, the NHS now employs nurses not GPs to provide out of hours care. In some towns with six figure populations there is only one doctor on call at night. Patients who call for a GP in the middle of the night have to make do with a nurse. In England, there are now whole counties with just three doctors providing cover at night. Nurses are usually very good at plumping up pillows and taking temperatures but they are not trained as diagnosticians in the way that doctors are supposed to be, nor are they trained to treat patients. Sending a nurse out to deal with emergency patient problems is akin to the fire brigade sending out a telephone operator to deal with a fire. It seems obvious to anyone other than those running the NHS that triage (deciding who needs the most urgent treatment) should be conducted by the most highly trained individuals. This was what GPs did before the Government agreed to let them stop working at nights and weekends. It is sadly true that doctors make too many mistakes, but allowing the least well-trained, least experienced employees to make the most important decisions is madness. During 2006, complaints about the out of hours service provided by the NHS rose by a fifth. Common criticisms included failing to diagnose conditions properly and delaying in visiting patients. At least 35 people died because of failings in out of hours care in 2006.

★ ★ ★

1. Cleaners at an NHS hospital were told to turn over dirty sheets instead of using fresh ones between patients. An NHS hospital, which had recorded 36 cases of MRSA and 327 cases of patients infected with clostridium difficile in less than a year, asked staff to reuse dirty sheets in order to save money.

2. A 76-year-old woman suddenly and inexplicably went blind in one eye. Terrified, she rang her doctor. A voice told her that she could see someone in four weeks time. (The awful thing is that we don't even blink when we hear horror stories of this type. We don't question their truthfulness because we know in our hearts that they are true.)

3. Patients living in England who suffer from age-related macular

degeneration aren't given the drug that would stop them going blind. In Oxfordshire, for example, the local branch of the NHS, claims that it considers funding to treat the condition in exceptional cases. At the time of writing it had, however, turned down every one of 71 applications that have been made. All patients in Gordon Brown's home country of Scotland get the drug but in England only one in five patients receive it – and then only after they have gone blind in one eye. As a result of this blatant discrimination against the English more than 20,000 Englishmen and women will go blind every year.

4. Each year 7,800 patients are diagnosed with head and neck cancer. If they live in Gordon Brown's home country of Scotland they will be treated. But if they live in England they are denied a new drug that will enable them to survive for, on average, over four years. The Government has decided that it is more cost effective to let English patients die than it is to treat them. Patients in Scotland are saved with money provided by English taxpayers.

5. A baby with a fractured skull was left crying for 90 minutes in a hospital waiting room. When no nurse or doctor came to see him his parents took their baby to another hospital. By that time he was vomiting and losing consciousness. A scan showed that he had a fractured skull and a massive blood clot on his brain. Would Mr and Mrs Gordon Brown have to wait 90 minutes if they took their child to hospital in similar circumstances?

6. In 2006, the NHS paid out £592,000,000 in compensation over blunders. A third of that was paid to lawyers.

7. Hospitals treat patients with bunions before they treat patients with cancer because bunions are easier and quicker to deal with and so bring down the hospital's overall waiting time. This enables administrators to meet their artificial targets. Despite this chicanery half a million people are still spending more than a year waiting to be treated. One in eight patients now treated in British hospitals has waited more than twelve months.

8. Here's another trick hospitals have thought up to help meet Gordon's stupid targets. You need an operation. You're on

a waiting list. A nurse or a clerk asks you when you're on holiday. Thinking that this is sensible of them, you tell them when you're away. And that's when they send you the appointment telling you that you can have your operation. Because you're away you don't reply or turn up and the hospital can deal with someone else. But by sending you an appointment they've dealt with you. Two patients are taken off the waiting list. You go to the bottom of the list and start waiting again. Brilliant.

9. Thousands of patients with prostate cancer are being given potentially dangerous drugs quite unnecessarily just to meet targets and clear hospital waiting lists. The best course of action with prostate cancer patients is sometimes to do nothing – to wait and see what happens before deciding on the best course of treatment. (Often no treatment at all is the best treatment.) But Government targets mean that all patients have to be treated within four weeks. And so although some patients are denied the drugs they need other patients are given drugs they don't need. All thanks to Gordon's performance targets.

★ ★ ★

How many deaths is Gordon Brown responsible for?

I have no idea. Nor, I suspect, has he.

While the Government claims that it is meeting targets in the NHS the truth is that rapidly increasing numbers of people are using their savings to pay for private treatment in order to avoid life-threatening delays and filthy hospital wards. Thanks largely to Gordon Brown a whole industry has grown up helping Britons go abroad to get medical treatment they've already paid for in the UK. There are now 500 companies in Britain involved in helping patients get medical treatment abroad and the industry, which is growing by 50% a year, is now worth nearly £200 million a year. Patients go to Hungary, India, Turkey and Thailand because hospitals there are cleaner and more efficient. In 2006, well over 50,000 British taxpayers went abroad for treatment. Some went simply hoping to have their hips done before they died. Some went because they wanted to increase their chances of staying alive.

★ ★ ★

Similar things happen in the world of education. In order to satisfy Gordon's absurd targets (and therefore show that they are doing their jobs properly according to Gordon's requirements) schools have to get more students to pass examinations and to go to university.

The inevitable has happened: the standard of exams has been lowered to make sure that more students pass them every year. And so, while employees complain that school leavers are barely literate or numerate, the Government is able to claim that schools are performing marvels.

After ten years of Brownian targets nearly half of all school leavers in Britain are functionally illiterate. Could there, just possibly, be a link between that and the Teachers' Workloads Survey which showed that primary school teachers spend more time doing Gordon's paperwork than they do teaching core subjects such as history, geography, music and physical exercise combined. Similarly, in secondary schools, teachers spend less time teaching key subjects than they spend on office work. In the summer of 2007, it was reported that nearly half of all Britain's children still can't read, write or do simple sums by the time they reach the age of eleven. How ironic it is that Gordon Brown should have come to power in 1997 on an election platform based on Tony Blair's priority promise of 'education, education, education'. (This mantra was, in fact, stolen from the former East Germany's communist regime.) I suppose the good news, as far as Gordon is concerned, is that half of all school leavers now and in the future will be unable to read this book.

> The Labour Party has decided to deny university places to the children of graduates. This is social engineering at its rawest and most unfair. It is blatant discrimination. Before long I suspect that universities in India and other Asian countries will start accepting English students who are, for family reasons, denied an education in their home country. This may sound unbelievable, but how many people would have expected Indian hospitals to be crowded with English patients seeking treatment abroad in order to avoid waiting lists, dirty hospitals, incompetence and rudeness?

The police have thought up tons of ways of fiddling their targets so as to meet the official Brownian requirements. So, for example, they reclassify real crimes as merely suspicious circumstances so that there are less crimes in their area. Or, if it's appropriate, they divide up crimes into lots of crimes so that they can improve their figures for solving crimes. 'We've recovered your handbag, madam. How many items are there in it? Just 97? Splendid. Thank you. That's 97 crimes solved.'

You think I'm kidding don't you?

I'm not.

Consider the true case of the boy who collected £700 for Comic Relief but failed to hand in the money. Because the money had been collected from 542 different people, Home Office Brownian rules stipulated that this allowed the police to log 542 crimes as solved.

This sounds rather funny in the cold light of day.

But, in reality, it isn't funny at all.

The police are making ludicrous arrests to meet Government targets. One policeman arrested a child who threw a slice of cucumber at a classmate, and a second charged two little girls with criminal damage after they drew flowers and hearts on a pavement with chalk. (The two girls were fined £80.) Dozens of armed policemen, assisted by dogs and helicopters, surrounded two teenage girls dressed as cowgirls with pink handled toy guns. The girls had been attending a cowboys and Indians fancy dress party. A man was cautioned for being 'in possession of an egg with intent to throw'. A child was arrested for throwing buns at a bus. Stallholders were fined £80 for selling T-shirts with the slogan 'Bollocks to Blair'. A woman was arrested on her wedding day for criminal damage to a car park barrier when her foot slipped on the accelerator. Police cautioned a man for throwing a glass of water over his girlfriend. Two children were arrested under gun laws for being in possession of a toy pistol. An 87-year-old man was sent four letters threatening to take him to court for allowing his car to be hit while it was (perfectly legally) parked. He was having lunch in a restaurant at the time. And, in a tribute to fascism, the police in Britain have even arrested a man for owning a book the Government didn't like. (When they start arresting people for owning books then we know we're in trouble. How many of the books on your shelf are likely to bring armed police round to your door?) A 23-year-old woman who ordered a CD by the well-known American rock band Anthrax, was having her hair done when a policeman burst in and arrested her under the Terrorism Act. She was handcuffed. There were three police cars and three police vans parked in the street outside. At the police station the police told her that a post office employee had opened an envelope she had posted. (No, I didn't know post office employees had been given the right to open the mail.) The post office employee had been shocked to find that the envelope contained a cheque for £6. Written on the back were the words 'Anthrax CD'. The police had arrested the woman because they thought she was ordering anthrax germs for a terrorism attack. The woman explained their mistake but was nevertheless kept in the cells overnight.

A spokesman for the police admitted: 'When people are being pushed to show results they will use anything they can to demonstrate they are doing a good job.' As a result of the targets they have to meet, the police in Britain are now 'owned' thoroughly by the Government. The fact that a politicised police force is a great danger to freedom and democracy is well-illustrated by the way that the police oppress the dwindling number of demonstrators who dare to oppose Government policy – often using legislation designed to curb terrorism.

When police searched an anti-war protestor who was carrying a placard they found that he had in his possession three copies of a Vanity Fair article entitled 'Blair's Big Brother Britain'. The police, with absolutely no sense of irony and seemingly quite unaware that their deeds they were confirming the truth of the accusation they would deny, decided that this was 'politically motivated' material and charged him under the Serious Organised Crime and Police Act. According to the police, carrying an article which questions the Government can now be regarded as evidence of criminal intent. The placard the man was carrying contained a quote from George Orwell: 'In a time of universal deceit telling the truth is a revolutionary act.' The demonstrator was, of course, found guilty.

> 'You're lucky to be living in a democracy!'
> Policeman talking to a citizen who had asked the police
> if they thought their response was excessive when they
> surrounded, jostled, pushed and threatened members
> of the public, including children and elderly people, who
> were attempting to release balloons bearing messages
> into the air. The man who dared to ask the question was
> wrestled to the ground by six officers, arrested, had a
> DNA sample taken and was given an £80 fine.

It is this sort of mentality that enables the Government to claim that it is winning the fight against crime when the public know that this is a lie. If the Government is winning the fight against crime how do Ministers explain the fact that millions of people no longer dare go out of their homes after dark?

★ ★ ★

The police, like every other organisation, business and individual in Britain today, spend much of their time filling in forms and completing paperwork. Partly thanks to the need to satisfy Brown's absurd targets, rather than deal with real problems and satisfy the genuine needs of taxpayers, we now live in a bureaucratic state. Just one small offence now requires 17 police officials and 131 pieces of paper. During Brown's ten years at the Treasury, the Labour Government introduced over 3,000 new criminal offences.

After ten years of Gordon Brown, Britain, home of target-driven policing, now has a higher crime rate than Denmark, Belgium, Germany, Netherlands, Finland, France, Austria, Luxembourg, Italy, Greece, Portugal, Spain, and Ireland. Britain is now the most burgled country in Europe and the levels of assault are the highest across the EU. The figures for car theft, robbery and sex offences are well above average in Britain. The European Crime and Safety Survey, a joint project involving the European Union Commission and the United Nations and described as 'the most comprehensive analysis of crime, security and safety ever conducted in the EU' showed that the percentage of households burgled was 3.3% in the UK and 1.6% in France. The average throughout the EU was 1.65%. The percentage of the population exposed to crime was 21% in the UK but 14.5% in the rest of Europe. Britain's crime rate is nearly three times as high as the crime rate in America, for heaven's sake. Despite this only 13 people go to prison in Britain for every 1,000 crimes committed. Put another way this means that after ten years of Brownian performance targets, 987 out of every 1,000 criminals remains free. This is a third of the success rate the police had half a century ago. Brown's philosophy of giving policemen targets to meet has failed miserably with the public losing out and criminals being the only victors. In a way this low success rate is probably a blessing for the Home Office. As a result of the thousands of draconian new laws that have been introduced during the last decade, the prison population in Britain has soared to more than 80,000 (up from 60,000 when Labour came to power). Many prisons are overcrowded and are having to turn customers away.

★ ★ ★

Brown has proved himself congenitally incapable of sticking to spending plans. He has wasted more taxpayers' money than any politician in history. His spending on public services has risen at an absurd rate. Between 1997 and 2007 he increased spending on education from £37 billion to £70 billion and he increased spending on the NHS from £35 billion to £92 billion. And yet, during his tenure, hospitals have been laying off staff, the armed forces have been starved of essential resources and the public service unions are screaming about inadequate pay rises. It is impossible to find any intelligent citizen who believes that the quality of public services has improved during Brown's tenure. On the contrary, there is clear evidence that everything has got worse – far worse. Education and health care are both in deep crisis. Children are cheated of a decent education and the sick are dying when they could be saved. There are over a million young Britons who are not in education, employment or training. They cost the taxpayer £3.6 billion a year. Every year tens of thousands of 16-year-olds leave school unable to read or write. More money than ever has been poured into public services. But it has been spent in the wrong way. Billions have been wasted on hiring administrators and bureaucrats when the money should have been spent on people trained, prepared and capable of doing real work. Brown is at least partly responsible for introducing thousands of new rules, regulations and targets and it is the targets which, more than anything, have done the damage. Public sector employees have spent their time finding ways to obey the rules and meet the targets. They have forgotten their real purpose – which is to serve the public.

Thanks to Gordon Brown, a recent UNICEF survey ranked the UK as one of the worst places in the world for children to live. The UNICEF report concluded that English children are the unhappiest in the Western world.

Millions of people now recognise that if you need to see a dentist, want to go into hospital (and avoid catching MRSA), would like your children to leave school literate, want to see a GP or would like to have your rubbish collected then you will have to 'go private'. Blair's legacy is the Iraq war. Brown's legacy is millions of people forced into debt to pay for basic services for which, as taxpayers, they have already paid.

Despite all the targets and all the careful measuring of performance, no Treasury forecast has been worth the paper that was wasted for its printing. And the Foreign Office has a well-deserved reputation for an utterly astonishing ability to misread situations, and to betray electors in favour of its own interests and the interests of the politicians. All Ministries are now so inept that the nation would be infinitely better run if politicians had the sense to make decisions as though every piece of advice received was the direct opposite to the truth.

The Government has missed 44 of the 101 targets set by Gordon Brown at the last spending review – according to the Government's own assessment of its performance.

Official inquiries into Governmental or civil service incompetence invariably end up with politicians and civil servants exonerated. Even when the finger of blame is pointing firmly in one direction the target will either be given a short holiday (gardening leave), promoted or excused.

Politicians lie, lie and lie again to protect themselves. Resignations are as rare as mares' nests. When things get unbearably bad politicians are promoted, either to the House of Lords or to the EU.

Chapter Five

Statist or Fascist?

'What, then, is the essence of fascism? It is the outcome of capitalism in decay. It is the retort of the propertied interests to a democracy which seeks to transcend the relations of production implied in a capitalist society...Success means using the state-power over the nation partly to coerce and partly to cajole it into acquiescence in his rule. That acquiescence is the sole purpose of, and the sole justification for, the methods that he uses. The only values he considers are those which seem likely to contribute to his success.'
HAROLD J LASKI, *REFLECTIONS OF THE REVOLUTION OF OUR TIME*

Gordon Brown is sometimes described as a 'statist'. I doubt if even his closest admirers could disagree with that description.

Statism is described in the dictionary as a political system in which the State has substantial central control over social and economic affairs. The word 'statism' accurately summarises the sort of policy favoured by New Labour for if ever there was a nation which could be described as statist it is Britain as it has been moulded by Brown. I cannot think of a significant British politician who has been more of a statist than Brown.

But the word 'statist' doesn't go quite far enough.

And the important question is: what, if anything, is the difference between statism, communism and fascism?

Communism is a political system in which all property is owned by the community. The word originated in 19th century France and is based on the principle of 'common property'. The communist system was, of course, best illustrated by the kind of government practised in the former Soviet Union. Gordon Brown's Britain is not a communist country. (Nor, since socialism is merely a slightly weakened version of communism, is Britain a socialist country.)

But what about fascism?

There is much confusion about precisely what fascism entails and the word is thrown around rather wildly as a term of abuse. Those who oppose the EU are dismissed as fascists. (Though the EU is probably the most perfectly fascist organisation in history) And politicians and commentators sometimes seem to suggest that fascism and racism are the same thing. (This simply isn't true. Fascism isn't racism. Mussolini's Italy was not racist).

It is, however, fairly simple to find a definition.

The official Oxford English Dictionary definition of a fascist is: 'One of a body of Italian nationalists organised in 1919 under Benito Mussolini to oppose Bolshevism.'

So, in order to find out what a fascist really is, all we need to do is find out what Mussolini meant by fascism.

Mussolini defined fascism as a political system in which the rights of the state expressed the real essence of the individual. And he went on to say that: 'We were the first to assert that the more complicated the forms of civilisation, the more restricted the freedom of the individual must become.'

It is, incidentally, assumed that fascism always comes from the right. But fascism can also come from the left. Indeed, today most fascism comes from the left. And there is absolutely no difference between the two varieties. To the victims it doesn't matter whether the fascism is created by right wingers or left wingers.

Fascism reduces our freedom and privacy because only the state really matters and the state (and those who work for it and control it) takes precedence over everyone and everything else.

In principle, the state exists to provide citizens with an infrastructure. To pay for this, the state is allowed to tax the electorate.

But this Government now uses the taxes it raises for other things (funding wars, hiring civil servants to vote Labour and hiring expensive spin-doctors to make the lies ever more convincing) so that there is virtually nothing left for the essential infrastructure.

The British Government now spends nearly half of the nation's Gross Domestic Product but it spends most of the money on the wrong things and so the country is falling apart.

In a fascist country the government doesn't nationalise the means of production because it doesn't need to. Instead it merely assumes total control through regulation and legislation. Small businesses, regarded as a dangerous sign of independence and freedom, are controlled by regulations and red tape. In other words, although fascism leaves ownership in the hands of individuals it gives effective control of those businesses to the state. But, of course, ownership without control is a contradiction and what this means in reality is that the individual has all the responsibility while the state has all the authority.

A fascist country is one where the state controls virtually everything; it is a country where the state bureaucrats decide what is good for the ordinary citizens; it is a country where the state makes all or most of the decisions about how money should be spent; it is a country where the state grabs most of the wealth and then doles the cash out in dribs and drabs. A fascist state is paternalism gone mad: everyone works and the state hands out pocket money. Fascism is the annihilation of democracy.

The UK, without doubt a fascist country, is now one of the most centralised political systems in the world. People have stopped bothering to vote because politicians no longer take any notice of them. Today, more people in Britain vote in television talent shows than vote in parliamentary elections. The subordination of the individual to the state is an integral part of fascism. The fascist has no real doctrine except a passionate desire to remain in authority.

People won't complain about what is going on because they have been institutionalised by the system – in the same way that prisoners or long-term hospital patients become institutionalised. Real people, with real passions, real interests in their community, have been replaced by apparatchiks, Labour Party gofers, hacks and professional expense claimers, people who once shared a train compartment with Tony Blair, people whose sole ability is to fill in forms and live within the system, for whom the system is the end rather than a form of management and people whose only real skills are perjury, fraud and extortion.

The Tories were bad enough, but Labour has finally shown us the extent to which politicians will go, just how dangerous they can be and how crucial it is to control their power.

We don't have a Prime Minister (in the sense that Winston Churchill was a Prime Minister). Instead we have a malevolent dictator, a man for whom most of us never voted in any election. We have politicians whose primary motive seems to be self-aggrandisement and self-enrichment rather than any sense of public service. The Government is anti-worker, anti poor, anti-peace, anti-freedom, anti-ambition and anti-democracy.

Modern politics is all about self-preservation and self glorification. It has nothing to do with the needs of the electorate or the country.

> If you are British there are now 266 laws giving Government-employed thugs power to enter your home. Britain has more public and private closed circuit television cameras per person than any other country in the world. The 4.2 million CCTV cameras work out at one for every 14 people.

In a fascist country it is the sick, the weak and the needy who suffer most and we are now seeing, at first hand, the institutionalised economic oppression of the masses by the state. Remember: fascism means that the state comes first and the people come a long way second. The state's employees exist to defend the state (rather than to care for the people) and that is why their loyalties are to the state. Civil servants whose working lives are dominated by the need to satisfy the state machinery by hitting performance targets are working not for the people but for the party machinery – the state.

The only honest purpose of a Government is to protect its citizens; to work for them.

But Brown has acted like a ruler not a servant and our individual rights have been eroded and replaced with state rights.

In a real democracy the state should have no rights; it should only have responsibilities. In a real democracy the Government should only be entitled to use force to protect the rights of the individual.

But our Government controls us with fear and force.

We have been destroyed by a potent and poisonous mixture of statism, fascism, multiculturalism, political correctness and political self-interest.

Fascism is effectively gang rule. Gangsters loot the efforts of productive citizens and constantly search for new ways to do so. Individual rights are ignored or suppressed. The people are controlled by laws, by regulations and by fear.

In a democratic country, the state has responsibilities to the individual. The state collects money from individuals (through taxes) and then uses that money to provide an infrastructure.

But in our utterly fascist society the state accepts no responsibilities. Instead, the state makes up unfair, unreasonable, laws. And collects money to sustain itself, its hierarchy and their thugs.

Chapter Six

The Imprudent Chancellor And The Worst Budget Deficit In Western Europe

'Confound not the distinctions of thy Life which Nature hath divided, that is, Youth, Adolescence, Manhood and old Age; nor in these divided Periods, wherein thou art in a manner Four, conceive thyself but One. Let every division be happy in its proper Virtues, nor one Vice run through all. Let each distinction have its salutary transition, and critically deliver thee from the imperfections of the former, so ordering the whole, that Prudence and Virtue may have the largest Section.'
SIR THOMAS BROWNE

The International Monetary Fund has warned that there is now a £58 billion hole in Britain's public finances. Forecasts from the Organisation for Economic Cooperation and Development show that Brown left the Treasury with the worst budget deficit in Western Europe. The shortfall between Government revenue and spending was 2.6% of gross domestic product in 2007. That is higher than any of the 30 OECD countries around the world except the USA and Japan. In Europe, only the Czech Republic and Hungary have higher shortfalls.

The Centre for Policy Studies claims that Britain's national debt is three times greater than the Treasury admits. The official

Treasury figure for the National Debt excludes the cost of public pensions liabilities, the hidden costs of Labour's Private Finance Initiative contracts and the debts incurred by Network Rail. The Centre says that if public sector pension liabilities and private finance initiative liabilities are added to total borrowings (as they obviously should be) the total Government debt accumulated by Scotsman Gordon Brown amounts to £1,340 billion and not the £486 billion which Brown claimed. This is higher than Britain's GDP and means if the national debt was shared out, every household in the UK would have to find £53,000. This is Gordon Brown's financial legacy to the nation. A massive debt. Thanks to Brown, Britain's economic future grows bleaker by the day.

Since 2001, the UK has moved from a small annual budget surplus to a 3% annual deficit. There has been no GDP growth at all. And yet our entire economy depends on growth.

As a result, Brown has left the nation in a perilous state. If Britain were an individual it would, thanks to Brown's policies, be bankrupt. It takes a special type of incompetence to combine the highest taxes in British history with the worst public services in the world and the worst public finances in Western Europe.

Under Gordon Brown's chancellorship the public spending ratio in the United Kingdom has overtaken Germany's for the first time. The British Government now takes, and spends, 46% of the national income.

All the main English-speaking economies have grown faster than the UK since 1997. And, around the world, many other countries are growing faster too. Excluding the obvious contenders (China and India) even countries such as Greece, Finland, Luxembourg, Iceland and Spain have faster growing economies.

During Gordon Brown's reign as Chancellor of the Exchequer the Labour Party's own debts rose to astronomical levels. At one point it was alleged that the party which was running the country owed £40 million. (The debts rose despite the 'loans' the party had received from generous donors who definitely didn't want to become peers.)

Britain now has a massive trade deficit.

A trade deficit occurs when a country imports more stuff than it exports. So, if a country imports more Chinese-made television sets and Japanese cameras than it exports tweed socks and pork pies it will have a trade deficit. This is just as much bad news as it would be if a household spent more than it had coming in. It is, in short, unsustainable. And, in the end, it will have to be corrected with a painful period of restraint.

Despite Gordon Brown's constant claims of prudence the fact is that after ten years with him as Chancellor, Britain's trade deficit has grown to mammoth proportions.

In 2006, Britain's trade deficit was £60 billion.

This may be peanuts compared to America's trade deficit. But it's still a deficit. It still means that the country is in debt. And it's yet another piece of evidence supporting my argument that Gordon Brown is the worst and most incompetent Chancellor Britain has ever had.

When a country has a trade deficit it must either borrow in order to survive or else rely on external investors putting money into the country. (Just as you or I would have to borrow or find a generous relative if we spent more than we earned.)

Our national debt is rising. And eventually someone is going to have to pay the bill. Our children, or our children's children are going to be very poor as they struggle to pay back the debts we built up by spending too much on foreign-made television sets and game consoles. Debts are debts and the Chinese aren't going to let Britain out of its obligations any more than your bank will let you out of your obligations if you run up a huge overdraft.

Britain has a trade deficit because our manufacturing industry is dying. Britain now has only two successful manufacturing sectors: arms and pharmaceuticals.

It is Britain's growing dependence on the pharmaceutical industry which explains Blair's change of view about vivisection. In 1997, the Labour Party wanted vivisection stopped – and regarded it as pointless and invalid, as well as cruel and immoral. By the early 21st century, the Labour Party was encouraging vivisection, vigorously defending vivisectors and introducing fistfuls of new laws outlawing opposition to animal experiments.

And it is our dependence on the success of our arms industry which partly explains Tony Blair's constant warmongering. If you aren't constantly killing people and blowing things up then the demand for fresh supplies of arms is rather limited.

Apart from arms and drugs, Britain now depends on money earned from management consultancy, public relations, advertising and financial services. As Larry Elliott and Dan Atkinson explain in their book *Fantasy Island*, 'we count the money and do the bullshit'.

Having a trade deficit matters because it means that the country as a whole has acquired bad habits.

We have become spending junkies.

And we aren't spending real money – money we've earned by making widgets and selling them to Indonesia.

Instead, we are spending money which we have borrowed.

And how come the banks have allowed us to borrow so much?

Easy.

As I explained earlier in this book, we've been borrowing against our rising house prices.

The snag (and there is, of course, a snag) is that when a country has a large trade deficit big pressure is put on the nation's currency.

Indeed, no country has ever run a deficit of more than 5% without there being a huge drop in the value of its currency. By huge I mean at least 30%.

The reason for this is simple.

When a country is in debt its own currency becomes dodgy. And, of course, it needs foreign currency to pay off the foreign debts.

Inevitably, the Labour Government claims that none of this matters.

Britain is, they say, a knowledge economy. Their philosophy is: 'We can supply the brains and we will let someone else do the dirty work.'

In other words, Britons will invent new television sets and get other people to make them. Then we'll take a big chunk of the profits.

But there are (inevitably) several flaws in this argument.

First, our rising knowledge economy (providing financial and advertising services to the rest of the world) is nowhere near big enough to pay for our buying habits. We aren't counting enough money or doing enough bullshit.

Second, most research and development in an economy is driven (and paid for) by manufacturing industry. New ideas for new products arise when a country is constantly making things. When a country doesn't have much of a manufacturing industry it doesn't do much research or developing of new products. In other words, tomorrow's goods will doubtless be made in China but they will be designed there too. We are out of the loop. We aren't making things any more and we aren't getting other people to make things we've invented either. Our colleges and universities aren't training engineers. Instead, they are training people in nail technology and pub management.

Which takes us back to our national reliance on our service industry: advertising, banking and so on.

And the real problem is that our service industry isn't bringing in enough foreign money any more. And that's because the fastest growing occupation in Britain isn't in advertising or management consultancy or banking.

It's hairdressing.

Our service industry – the only bit of the economy which is still growing and still making money – is crimping and perming so that we can all look nice for one another.

And, sadly, the Chinese aren't flying over here to get their hair done.

We aren't even a nation of shopkeepers any more. We have become a nation of bloody hairdressers.

★ ★ ★

But It isn't just the nation which is in debt. The average Briton now has twice as much unsecured debt as the average European. In 2005, Britons took on £215 billion of personal debt – more than a third of the £600 billion borrowed by everyone in continental Europe.

Including mortgage debts, the total consumer debt in Britain exceeds £1.3 trillion – close to three times the level of borrowing in 1997 when Gordon Brown first took over at the Treasury.

When Brown first came to power Britons borrowed the same amount as their income. Today Britons borrow one-and-a-half times their income. The typical borrower spends 51% of his monthly pay on mortgage repayments. Personal bankruptcies are soaring and so is the number of mortgage borrowers missing repayments on their loans. There are 250,000 bankruptcies and insolvencies a year in England and Wales.

Bankruptcy is the nation's second growth industry. (Second, of course, to hairdressing.)

Chapter Seven
The Architect Of Britain's Housing Crisis

'The way to stop financial joy-riding is to arrest the chauffeur,
not the automobile '
WOODROW WILSON

Britain's low interest rates (excused by the falsely low inflation figures Gordon Brown has foisted on the nation) have helped push up the stock market and house prices. As house prices have risen so people have had more money to spend. How? Because millions have increased their mortgage borrowing as the value of their house has gone up. Interest rates have been so low that paying back the money has been no problem. And since house prices are expected to go up and up, and to stay up, what's the problem?

The rise in house prices has been so extraordinary (and so utterly, breathtakingly barmy) that in the early summer of 2007 there were more houses on the market at over £2 million than there were on the market at under £100,000. A one bedroom flat in Belgravia, London was put on the market with an asking price of £3 million. The number of property millionaires in the UK (that is, people who have become millionaires solely because of the rise in the value of their home) rose by a third from 2005 to 2006. The proportion of houses fetching £1 million or more has increased tenfold since Labour came to power in 1997.

Everywhere you look there are figures which prove quite conclusively that house prices have risen to unsustainable levels.

Under Gordon Brown's management house ownership in Britain has been the closest thing imaginable to a mass lottery win. House prices in Britain have risen faster and further than anywhere else in the world and, as a result, London is now the most expensive city on the planet. Property in central London is now more expensive than property in Monaco.

There are several reasons for this.

First, as a result of Labour's policies the amount of immigration has rocketed. For every Briton who leaves at least two immigrants come in. This has dramatically increased the demand for housing. (Naturally, Labour Party supporters say that even mentioning this is akin to racism.)

Second, the amount of regulation and red tape introduced by Labour has made it much harder for building companies to get planning permission to build new houses. The Government keeps saying that Britain needs more housing. But everything it does makes house building more difficult, more expensive and more time consuming.

Third, Labour has done everything it can to destroy the family. There are now real financial incentives for people to live alone. The obvious result has been an increase in the demand for housing.

Fourth, by constantly printing more and more money to pay for its expensive expansion of the State, the Labour Government has dramatically decreased the value of the British pound. When the pound goes down in value everything else goes up. That's what inflation is. When interest rates are kept low while the amount of money produced is dramatically increased the consequences are inevitable: house price inflation.

Fifth, lenders have become absurdly aggressive – almost forcing barrowloads of money on borrowers and in so doing have laid the foundations for a serious crash. Banks are lending 120% of the cost of a property. Mortgages can be obtained for five times earnings – instead of the traditional three times earnings. Mortgages can now be obtained for periods in excess of half a century. There is now an industry of people selling fake pay slips so that people can persuade their mortgage lender to let them have a bigger loan than they might otherwise think wise. If you're unemployed but want a fake pay slip to show that you have a £50,000 a year job with a blue-chip company you just type 'duplicate pay slip' into an Internet search engine and choose your 'discreet and confidential' adviser. Then, take your evidence to the bank and come away with a loan for a quarter of a million pounds. This way lies bankruptcy and disaster.

And finally, since Brown deliberately and cold-bloodedly destroyed pensions for those Britons not employed by the Government, more and more people have been putting their savings into property rather than pension funds.

The result has been that Labour has, partly deliberately and partly through incompetence and stupidity, forced a tremendous increase in house prices. Gordon, being a moron, has undoubtedly welcomed the housing bubble. It is, after all, the dramatic and rather absurd increase in house prices which has given the nation the false growth it needs to pay for Gordon's mania for spending.

The rapid and nonsensical rise in house prices has, by itself, been dangerous enough. (House price rises are nonsensical because houses don't produce more as they age. Why should their value increase above inflation? This is unreal money.) Massive house price inflation has moved money from the poor to the rich and from the young to the old. It has created multimillionaires and billionaires out of property speculators. And, since much of the house price inflation has been confined to the South East of England it has divided the nation.

But there is worse.

The absurd and dramatic rise in house prices has created a massive consumer boom.

House owners have been borrowing money against the rising value of their homes. They have then been spending that money and pushing up the price of shares, art and just about everything else they can lay their hands on. And the Government has regarded all that spending as a sign of growth in the economy. It isn't growth, of course. It's debt. And it has partly explained the apparent boom that has taken place under Labour.

This hasn't just happened in the UK. It's been a global phenomenon. In America there has been an identical boom.

Average wages haven't risen in the USA for a staggering 30 years. The consumer boom there has been entirely led by the rise in house prices. In Japan, banks have been lending money at interest rates as low as 0%. They have, in other words, been giving money away to encourage spending.

Every time the Bank of England pushes up interest rates (in a belated attempt to cool the economy, dampen spending and weaken the over-heated housing market) the pound rises on the international markets. As a direct result, foreign money floods into Britain because investors in other countries want to take advantage of our higher interest rates. This new money has to be put to work. And so the bankers who have taken it lend it out. And so there is more money available for people wanting to buy houses. And so house prices continue to rocket.

During 2007, as interest rates rose, some so-called experts claimed that high interest rates were good for landlords because first time buyers would be forced out of the market, making them rent instead. This nonsense comforted the idiots continuing to purchase overpriced properties. By June 2007, the typical residential property in the UK was producing a gross yield of around 5.5%. After costs this meant the landlords were receiving around 3.5% on their investments. Since most buy-to-let mortgages were costing 6% this meant that the average buy-to-let house owner was losing 2.5% on their investment every year. That's hardly the way to riches but, for the poor devils whose pensions had been utterly devastated by Brown's policies, a flat that is losing a bit of money a year is a darned sight better than a pension fund that is disappearing in front of your very eyes.

Before Brown destroyed pensions the buy-to-let market was about 1% of the whole housing market. After Brown destroyed pensions the buy-to-let market shot up to 10% of the whole market. A tenfold increase in the number of people buying houses and flats as an investment (rather than to live in themselves) has inevitably had a dramatic influence on house prices. Indeed, there is proof of this in that rental prices have remained stable whereas house prices have soared and are, compared to rental prices, now at least 50% overvalued.

The only sensible conclusion is that there is no real housing shortage. There is, on the other hand, a shortage of housing to buy because buy-to-let investors, putting their savings into property rather than pensions, have snapped up huge swathes of what is available.

The housing market is like a mass lottery win. Everyone who buys a house wins a huge prize. For much of the 21st century most homeowners were earning less through their work than their houses were earning for them. Even quite ordinary houses were increasing in value by £50,000 a year – tax free.

> A bull market in anything ends when everyone who can buy has bought. By that point most people honestly believe that the only way prices can go is up. It happens with shares. And now it has happened with houses.

When the bottom is reached (and most things that go up have a habit of coming down eventually) people will dismiss the idea of buying a house as lunacy. No one will want to buy houses. Property will be the worst asset to consider if you have some spare money. Young couples will talk only of renting and never of buying. When house prices start to collapse they will go down much further than seems sensible or logical. House prices have gone up too far. They will go down too far. They will go down too far because people will panic and they will sell at any price. And just as they lost touch with reality when prices were going up so they will lose touch with reality as prices come down. Greed took house prices up. (Though there was also the fear that if they didn't buy now then they would never be able to buy). Fear, and nothing but fear, will take prices down.

To those who consider their house as a home and not an investment then none of this matters. The *value* of their home is irrelevant. They bought it and they live in it. That's fine. But people who consider their houses to be an investment or pension are going to worry a good deal. People who bought at the top, with a massive bank loan, aren't going to have much choice. They will be lucky to get out with their coats.

Looking at the figures dispassionately it seems that, by mid

2007, property in Britain was at least 25% overvalued by every possible sensible criteria.

But this doesn't mean that if house prices fall they will fall by 25%.

When markets get out of kilter, as they do from time to time, and as they have under Gordon Brown's direction, the correction which invariably ensues always goes as far in the other direction.

So, if house prices are overvalued by 25% then the chances are that house prices will fall not by 25% but by 50%. A house currently worth £300,000 will, when the crash finally teeters to a conclusion, be worth £150,000. If a buyer can be found.

By then, of course, no one will be buying houses.

And renting will be quite cheap.

That's the chaos Gordon Brown has created.

Signs of a house price collapse are already in evidence. In June 2007, it was reported that there were more than 200 companies which had been set up specifically to buy houses at discounted prices from distressed home owners. In some instances the companies were renting the houses back to the sellers. Many of the companies were buying homes at 70-80% of their market value and then renting back the houses at less than the previous monthly payments. A year earlier there were just 20 or so such companies.

But even the professionals are making mistakes. Property dealers recently spent $39 billion buying a large and impressive looking building. They bought it with money costing them 6.5%. The yield on the property was capped (for the foreseeable future) at 3.75%. This was as daft as any investment by a buy-to-let investor. Both are gambling that the capital gain will cover the difference between income and the outgoings.

In the sensible old days, people bought investment property only when they could guarantee an income greater than the cost. Any capital gain was a bonus. Today the deals are being driven solely by the idea of massive capital gains.

★ ★ ★

Over half of London's multimillion pound homes are now bought not by Britons but by non-domiciled foreigners using

Britain as a tax haven. And over two thirds of properties sold for more than £5 million are sold to foreign buyers. London is the world's most attractive tax haven. (It is also the money laundering capital of the world.)

Thanks to Gordon Brown, foreigners have an added advantage over British buyers when buying houses. If they buy shares in an offshore firm that owns the London property, rather than buying the house directly, they pay stamp duty of 0.5% (the rate due on share purchases) rather than at 4% (the rate due on the purchase of houses costing more than £500,000). This cuts the tax bill on a £5 million house from £200,000 to £25,000.

The flood of foreign money coming into the London property market has driven the rest of the market up. Rich London buyers are forced out of the most desirable areas into less desirable parts of London, thereby pushing the price up in the area where they do buy. The successful British couple who have a couple of million to spend, and thought they would quite like a place in Knightsbridge, have to settle for Notting Hill because everything in Knightsbridge is being bought by foreigners who, because of Britain's generous tax deals, are at a huge advantage. And the couple who thought they could buy a nice place in Notting Hill for one and a half million can now only afford a place in Paddington. And the people who thought they would buy somewhere in Paddington can only afford somewhere in Isleworth. And the couple who were going to buy in Isleworth are forced out to Reading. And so it goes. Property prices are being pushed up from below (because of all those people putting their pension money into flats instead of pension funds) and they are being pulled up from above by all the foreigners buying expensive properties in London.

Gordon Brown (who used the housing rise as a money-making exercise by putting the stamp duty on houses up to 4%) is personally responsible for this bizarre state of affairs.

Another reason why Gordon is a moron.

Incidentally, it is a myth that house prices always go up and down with interest rates. In Japan, interest rates have been zero (or thereabouts) for years but house prices have fallen steadily.

Nor is it true that there is a link between house prices and the availability of property. Spanish builders built 800,000 flats and houses in 2006 (in comparison, strict planning regulations meant that less than 200,000 were built in Britain – many of those being, with the Government's encouragement, deliberately built on flood plains) but Spanish house prices continued to rocket.

Property prices are determined by location.

That's why estate agents talk about location, location and location being the three most important influences on house prices.

Residential property is cheap in Poland because no one wants to live there. (Seemingly, not even the Polish). But houses are expensive in London because Britain is a tax haven for foreigners.

★ ★ ★

When house prices collapse the real losers will be the people who have stretched their budgets, and borrowed up to their eyeballs, in order to get onto the house-buying ladder. The homes that are repossessed won't be the multimillion pound mansions but will be the homes of the poor, the disfavoured, the underprivileged, the elderly and the disabled; the people struggling to survive on minimum wages in bad neighbourhoods. The losers will be the people who thought they'd managed to touch the hem of the property-owning dream. The winners will, as they always have been under Gordon Brown, be the crafty, the sneaky and the mega-rich.

Chapter Eight

Strangling The Economy With Red Tape

'Britain has invented a new missile. It's called the civil servant – it doesn't work and it can't be fired.'
GENERAL SIR WALTER WALKER

The civil service has always specialised in producing problems. During the First World War, Lord Samuel, British Home Secretary for a while, complained that the civil service was always adept at finding a difficulty for every solution.

But Gordon Brown has presided over the greatest production of red tape in British history. It's not surprising, therefore, that Brown is, in the view of many, the most violently anti-small business Chancellor in history.

The red tape brought in during the first 10 years of Labour rule is costing British industry £55 billion a year, according to a report from the British Chambers of Commerce in early 2007. Since small businesses are crucial to the economic survival of the nation this is a dangerous policy.

From time to time the Government has announced plans to reduce the amount of regulation now stifling British business. Sadly, these attempts have been staggeringly unsuccessful. Legislation introduced in 2001 with the aim of simplifying things got rid of 27 regulations and added 600 new ones.

Today, of course, the red tape has, like some uncontrollable fungus, spread beyond business and has infiltrated daily home life. We are fined if we put our rubbish out on the wrong day or if we leave the lid up on our wheelie bin or if we put a piece of domestic rubbish (an unwanted envelope, perhaps) into a public rubbish bin. We are going to be forced to carry identity cards at all times. If we don't we will be heavily fined or put in prison. We are going to have our DNA taken and stored in a police database. We must all be finger printed if we want to have passports and travel abroad. The present and planned infringements on our freedom and privacy are seemingly endless.

Brown has helped create a world in which there are so many laws that I doubt if anyone (with the possible exception of Ministers who are driven everywhere and who never do any real work or make any decisions except about new laws) manages to get through a day without breaking at least one or two.

Vernon Coleman

Chapter Nine
Creating A Society Dependent Upon The State

'A democracy will continue to exist up until the time that voters discover that they can vote themselves generous gifts from the public treasury. From that moment on, the majority always votes for the candidates who promise the most benefits from the public treasury, with the result that every democracy will finally collapse due to loose fiscal policy, which is always followed by a dictatorship.'
ALEXANDER TYLER, HISTORY PROFESSOR
AT UNIVERSITY OF EDINBURGH, IN 1787

Brown has created a society which is utterly dependent upon the state. Millions are unemployed or dependent on state handouts and benefits. The real unemployment figure in Britain is now 5.4 million and not the 1.7 million claimed by the Government's spin-doctors.

Millions of people choose to claim benefits rather than take jobs because they are better off on benefits than they would be if they worked. A hard working couple earning £24,000 are, after tax, just £4 a week better off than a single mother living on benefits. (Here is yet more evidence that the Government is, for its own political reasons, determined to destroy the family unit.)

> Scotland, Northern Ireland and Wales all take far more out of the economy than they contribute. In all these areas at least two thirds of the regional income is provided by the Government. This is, of course, unsustainable. Taxpayers in England are subsidising the rest of the United Kingdom.

Thanks to Gordon Brown, seven million households in Britain are now dependent on benefits for at least half their income. That means that more than one in three households are reliant on their working neighbours for their bread, their petrol, their beer and their cigarettes.

Among single parent families the figure rises to two thirds. Two out of three single parent families get all or most of their income from taxpayers.

Not since the slump of the 1930s have there been so many households dependent on means-tested benefits.

Put together, all this means that half the country is now dependent on money from the other half. It is as though every working man and woman in the country had to go through their daily working lives with a stranger hanging around their necks, demanding to be fed, clothed and housed.

People are now more than ever likely to expect the Government to solve all their problems rather than to use their skills and energies to look after themselves.

Under Gordon Brown's supervision the national bill for social security has risen to a record £160 billion a year and the Department of Work and Pensions now employs 125,000 people to hand the money out. This makes the Department of Work and Pensions a bigger employer than the Army. (I have long felt that it would be cheaper and more effective for the Government to put dustbins full of money on street corners every Friday and to invite people to help themselves to what they need.)

Did all this happen by accident?

I don't think so.

Although the money handed out in benefits comes from taxpayers it is handed out by the Government. And, inevitably,

74

this means that for many people the Government is the Family Provider. Millions of people in Britain are now utterly, totally dependent on the Government for their daily bread.

And to that figure you must add the seven million whose regular pay cheque comes from the Government.

None of this is an accident.

It has all happened because Gordon Brown is a statist.

And he knows that people who get their bread from the Government are likely to be loyal to it.

> Britain has the largest percentage of economically inactive men of any country in Europe.

Under Gordon Brown, Britain has seen one of the biggest surges in long-term sickness claims of any major world economy, according to the Organisation for Economic Cooperation and Development.

Hundreds of thousands of perfectly fit people have been pushed into claiming sickness benefits in order to hide the level of unemployment (which is, despite all the trickery, now officially up to 1.7 million).

The facts relating to Britain's benefits programme are staggering.

1. Even ministers have admitted that two thirds of the millions of Britons claiming incapacity benefit are fit to go back to work.

2. Around 40% of those who say they are too sick to work are at home because of mental health problems rather than physical disability.

3. Vast armies of policemen and firemen have taken early retirement because they claim they couldn't cope with the mental stresses involved in seeing cars collide or houses burning.

4. Since Gordon took over as Chancellor the number of people receiving incapacity benefit for five years or more has increased by 20 times.

5. The official cost of fraud in the benefits system is £2.6 billion a year. The unofficial figure is undoubtedly considerably higher than this.

6. An astonishing 8% of the British working age population are now on sickness related schemes. (The average in the 30 countries in the OECD is 6%).

New maternity leave and working rights legislation has put small employers in an impossible position. By law, mothers are now entitled to 12 months statutory maternity leave. Paid maternity leave has been extended to nine months. Employees who have children are now entitled to demand to be allowed to work reduced hours when (or if) they do decide to return to work. Employers who do not agree to this may find themselves stumping up damages.

The Government wants to give fathers the chance to take six months off work too. Parents are being given dramatically enhanced powers. The Government is giving parents the freedom to be late or not to go to work at all if a child is poorly. And they want parents to be given time off work to attend school plays and other social events.

Jobs have to be kept open for parents who take maternity or paternity leave. This puts an intolerable burden on owners of small businesses who must find some way to cope without a key worker for months on end.

Many who don't have children think that Gordon and his chums have gone too far and are creating serious new problems in society.

Those who disagree with this level of generosity point out that people who have children choose to do so and ask why the State and employers (and taxpayers and other employees) should pay, in so many ways, for this choice?

The Government has driven a huge wedge between those who have children and those who don't. One result is that many small employers now do everything they legally can to avoid hiring women of child-bearing age. Another result is resentment from employees who don't have children and who are not allowed to have time off work to deal with emergencies at home or to cope with a sick pet.

Chapter Ten
Selling Off The Family Gold At Rock-bottom Prices

'You have to choose (as a voter) between trusting the natural stability of gold and the honest and intelligence of members of government. And with due respect to those gentlemen, I advise you, as long as the capitalist system lasts, to vote for gold.'
GEORGE BERNARD SHAW

Governments used to back their currencies with gold. But these days they don't.

Prior to August 15th 1971, the world's money system was based on gold. Currencies couldn't float too high because the bits of paper that governments produced had to be backed by gold, kept in the relevant government vaults.

However, in 1971, Richard Nixon, the President of the USA, abandoned the historic link between gold and America's paper currency. On August 14th 1971, you could take your dollar note along to the American Treasury and exchange it for gold. On August 16th, the piece of paper was all you got and all they were going to give you.

This apparently simple act changed the world.

Today, governments no longer try to back what they print with stores of gold bullion. America, in particular, prints money as fast as the presses will go so that it can continue to pay its armies and attempt to take over the world. As a result the world now floats on a sea of American liquidity. Other countries don't want their currencies to rise too much against the dollar (or they will be at a commercial disadvantage and their products will cost too much when sold to Americans) so they print more of their currencies too. So, while the printing presses in America are churning out dollars, so the printing presses in Japan are churning out yen, the printing presses in Switzerland are churning out Swiss francs, the printing presses throughout Europe are churning out euros and the printing presses in Britain are churning out pounds sterling.

It is this sea of paper money that has, inevitably, pushed up global property prices. Indeed, the price of everything collectible has gone up. Old cars, art, wine, rare watches, land, books – they have all risen in price as people realise that it is much better to own something tangible than to own suitcases full of paper money that isn't really worth anything.

We can't blame Brown for taking Britain's currency away from gold (that happened a long time ago) but, amazingly, one of the first things Gordon did when he got to the Treasury in 1997 was to sell off much of what was left of the nation's store of gold.

During his decade as Chancellor of the Exchequer, Gordon Brown did many things that could be described as wicked and a number of things that could be described as stupid. But one of the most painfully, egregiously, predictably stupid things he did was to sell off more than half of Britain's gold reserves. Brown sold 400 tons of our gold between 1999 and 2002, when the gold price was at a twenty year low. Brown allegedly ignored advice not to sell from experts at the Bank of England. Since Brown sold the nation's gold the price has tripled.

This single act of rank incompetence cost Britain over £2 billion.

Brown actually made things worse for the nation by auctioning the gold instead of selling it quietly through the usual channels. By letting the financial world know what he was doing Brown made sure that the gold was sold at the lowest possible price.

It is rumoured that Brown sold the gold so as to buy euros in order to please the Labour Party's friends in the EU. As a result of the sale, Britain now has the poorest gold assets of any Western country. The USA has 8,133 tons of gold. France has 2,710 tons of gold. Germany has 2,422 tons of gold. Britain now has just 315 tons.

Brown sold at a time when many experts realised that the price of gold could really only go upwards because the price of the metal had fallen so low that it was no longer profitable to dig the stuff out of mines. A shortage, and a rise in price, was inevitable.

Chapter Eleven

Tax Credits: A Tool For A Control Freak

'One day the whole of Europe will be one vast socialist state
...even England.'
LENIN

Gordon Brown is a classic control freak. He wants to control every aspect of our lives. Tax credits are one of his favourite ways of controlling people. They are also an utter fiasco. And an expensive fiasco too.

The system of giving tax credits (rather than simply reducing taxes that have to be paid) is loved by Gordon. It means that he gets to control our money and to force us to do what he wants us to do. His patronising, statist system of tax credits, means-testing and handouts is every bit as patronising as the soup kitchens of Victorian England. The only difference is that the soup kitchens were run by kind-hearted people who meant well. Gordon's system is designed to encourage dependence on the State and, in that, it has been enormously effective. It has created a whole generation of people who were brought up on money given to them by the State and who regard State subsidies as their birthright. Gordon's tax credits have made it more profitable for thousands to work part time rather than full time.

Apart from this problem (big enough you might think) Gordon's tax credits scheme has turned out to be expensive and inefficient. Like almost everything else managed by the Government it has been handled with almost unbelievable levels of incompetence. The scheme is so complex that millions of individuals have received the incorrect amount of benefit and one ex-welfare reform minister has claimed that the cost of the disaster has added the equivalence of five pence onto income tax. In the summer of 2007, the Government admitted that it might have to write off billions of pounds of taxpayers' money paid out in error as tax credits – either overpaid or handed out by mistake. It turned out that the Treasury had demanded billions back, eventually taking 38,000 families to court in an attempt to claw back at least some of the overpayments. Not surprisingly, some of the money had been spent and Brown's department doubtless ended up with armfuls of TV sets and stereos.

No one at the Treasury seemed to know exactly how much had been paid out or lost. One estimate was that between 2003 and 2006 Brown's department had overpaid £5.8 billion in child and working tax credits and had paid out another £3.6 billion through fraud or error – making a total of £9.4 billion which had been lost. It was clear that much of that would never be recovered though in a decent world it would have been deducted from the salaries of the people who had so egregiously mismanaged the scheme. Incidentally, while many people were mistakenly given too much money, around 900,000 were underpaid. In the end the National Audit Office (not exactly the most onerous taskmaster) actually refused to sign off HM Revenue and Customs (HMRC) accounts because the errors were too huge for even them to stomach. Distress, chaos and wasted money was the end result of the bungling Brown's determination to interfere in our lives.

Today, not surprisingly, there are huge doubts about the validity of the whole scheme.

Tax credits mean that a single mother on minimum wage can now earn as much working 16 hours a week as a two-parent family, also on minimum wage, working 116 hours in a week. The whole scheme is so complicated that millions of man-hours are wasted understanding and managing it.

The Government's bizarre and disastrous childcare vouchers

scheme is yet another example of Gordon Brown's blisteringly glaring incompetence.

The voucher scheme exists to allow parents tax relief on childcare costs of up to £55 a week. But the relief isn't just offered on Government registered childminders or nurseries. Any form of supervised activity that isn't provided during compulsory school hours qualifies for the vouchers, and an individual is officially a child until the September following their 15th birthday. The result is that this stupid, stupid scheme allows parents to claim tax relief on piano lessons and tennis lessons. Even skiing lessons count for tax relief.

And since both parents can apply, households can claim £55 x 2 x 52 in tax relief. This means that childless taxpayers are paying thousands so that rich kids can have piano, tennis and skiing lessons.

So, Gordon is using taxpayers' money to teach rich kids how to ski.

Is that really what Brown intended?

If so then the man is a moron.

If it isn't what he intended then he is still a moron.

Another of Gordon's little schemes, pension credit, is so complicated that an estimated 1.6 million needy pensioners aren't claiming money to which they are entitled.

Chapter Twelve

Destroyer Of Family Life

'Marriage is a great institution — no family should be without it.'
BOB HOPE

Gordon has created a tax regime which discourages marriage and encourages single parent families; his taxes and benefits system are designed to favour lone parents — and to encourage parents who aren't single to say they are. The Government's own figures show that there are 1.9 million single parents in the UK but there are 2.1 million sole parents claiming benefits or tax credits. That means that 200,000 are cheating because of the advantages involved in not being married and not having a partner. Amazingly, in Gordon's Brave New Britain, parents who earn less than £50,000 a year would be better off splitting up.

The family is the basis of our civilisation but, I suspect for his own political reasons, Gordon Brown seems to have done his best to destroy it and replace the family with the State. Thanks to Gordon the number of British adults choosing to marry has fallen to the lowest level since 1862.

Is it possible that the main reason for Gordon's apparent antipathy towards marriage is a hope that by destroying marriage he will make it easier for the State to control people's lives? Without family units we all become loners and as loners we are more vulnerable to the threats and pressures of the State machine.

Whatever the reason, the terrible result is that after ten years with Gordon as Chancellor, British children are suffering.

British children are, to Gordon's eternal shame, the worst off children anywhere in the world's 21 richest nations. The statistics show that children are better off and better cared for in many much less prosperous countries. For example, children now do better in Hungary, Greece, Poland and the Czech Republic.

British children are most likely to be drunk at the age of 11, they are most likely to have had sex before they reach the age of 15 and they have the worst eating habits. As far as education is concerned, British children now come 17th out of 21 after ten years with Gordon at the financial helm. The rate of teenage births in Britain is the highest in the developed world.

Can we really tie all this into Gordon's tax policies?

Yes.

UNICEF, which produced the report I've quoted, has blamed the Labour Government for taking tax breaks away from married couples and, thereby, encouraging single mothers.

UNICEF says there is a link between single parent families and poor health and poor education.

Gordon isn't just a moron.

He's a nasty moron.

Vernon Coleman

Chapter Thirteen
The Sinking Ship

'We are fast approaching the stage of the ultimate inversion: the stage where the government is free to do anything it pleases, while citizens may act only by permission; which is the stage of the darkest periods of human history, the stage of rule by brute force.'
AYN RAND

Brown's tax-the-middle-classes-till-they-bleed policies (and his Government's failure to spend the money wisely, to provide a decent infrastructure or to maintain any respect for the basic principles of freedom and democracy) have resulted in the fact that every year around 300,000 Britons are leaving Britain and moving abroad. That figure is rising rapidly. (More people left the UK in 2006 than had left in any year since records began. The official figures for emigrating Britons was 385,000. In the same period the official figure for people coming into Britain was just under 600,000 – many from Eastern European countries. Illegal entrants aren't officially counted, of course.)

The people quitting the country are going to Australia, New Zealand, France, Spain, South Africa and Italy. They're going everywhere. And, contrary to the sort of drivel peddled in many of the newspapers, they aren't quitting in search of sunshine.

Every year a third of a million Britons leave the country because they can no longer stand living in Britain. While asylum seekers pour in to take advantage of what is left of the NHS, and to use the nation's absurdly generous benefits programme, several hundred thousand hard-working locals decide they've had enough and are going to sell up and live somewhere else. They're fed up with a Government which lies and cheats, which favours immigrants over native born Britons, which has destroyed the nation's infrastructure and which constantly raised taxes to a point where working and saving have become pretty pointless.

Now, what sort of people do you think these 300,000 emigrants are?

Are they Government employees, civil servants, who've had enough of working 35 hours a week for huge salaries and guaranteed index-linked pensions? No.

Are they the millions who are living carefree lives on unemployment benefits or disability benefits? No.

The people who are emigrating in such huge numbers are the hard-working, salt-of-the-earth Britons who have been taxed and bullied into submission by Brown. Hard-working, middle-class entrepreneurial Englishmen and women have been leaving their country in droves. These people are not leaving because they hate their country; they are leaving because they love their country and cannot stand what is being done to it.

While the Labour Government's policies encourage mass immigration (and, in particular, immigration by rich non-taxpayers) its policies also encourage mass emigration.

Thousands of businesses have been closed as their owners have moved abroad.

The emigrating Britons have not gone in search of sunshine. They have gone because life in the fascist country created by Brown et al has become intolerable.

If Brown was brighter he would realise that as the wealthy leave Britain so the tax burden on those remaining increases dramatically. Brown's policies have permanently damaged Britain's economic profile.

After ten years of Gordon Brown there are now nearly 5 million Britons living abroad. A recent survey showed that 78% of citizens born in Britain would leave the country if they could.

According to the Economist Intelligence Unit, approximately one in seven of Britain's richest people are already planning to move abroad to escape Britain's high taxes, absurd regulatory schemes and high living costs. A medical recruitment firm has reported that in the last twelve months it has received 1,000 enquiries from British doctors looking for work abroad. The previous year the firm received just 50 similar enquiries.

The ten most popular countries for exiled Britons running away from Gordon Brown are:

1. China 798,800
2. Australia 615,500
3. USA 527,500
4. Canada 232,699
5. New Zealand 215,900
6. France 206,200
7. South Africa 174,600
8. Spain 195,000
9. Ireland 108,900
10. Netherlands 78,500
11. Switzerland 72,200
12. Cyprus 63,800

(The numbers are the number of Britons now living in each country.)

Politicians don't care two hoots about this. They jeer and sneer and dismiss the emigrants as grannies tottering off in search of a bit of sunshine in Marbella.

How wrong can you be? How stupid can you be?

If the politicians actually looked at who is being driven abroad by Brown's policies they would see that many who quit are in their 30s, 40s and 50s. They aren't going to retire and to sit in the sunshine. They are going to try to find a country which treats its citizens with respect. They are going to countries where it is possible to start a new business without it being suffocated by red tape. They are going in search of a country where taxpayers get something back for their money. They are tearing up their roots and taking their families abroad to start again.

No country can afford to lose citizens of this type. These are the people who create a nation's wealth. They are the entrepreneurs, the inventors and the small business people whose work and ingenuity provides the finance for the civil servants and for the millions living on the benefits system.

With stultifying stupidity, utterly mind-boggling idiocy, Brown has driven abroad the very people who have paid for his multicultural, politically correct society.

Naturally, Brown never concerns himself with the people who are leaving. The Labour Party never asks people why they are emigrating and if they ever intend to come back.

And yet these are crucial questions.

The people who are quitting are, on the whole, people who have made a success of their lives in Britain. They usually own their own homes, often run their own businesses, and they invariably have some savings. They often have skills which are now in short supply. The people leaving are taxpayers; net contributors to the national budget. Their loss is a serious problem.

But no one in the Government cares enough even to make any basic enquiries about where they are going, why they are going, what they are looking for and what has caused their disillusionment. And, make no mistake about it, these people are disillusioned.

People don't sell everything, leave all their friends and relatives and go to live in a foreign country just because the weather is better. (Actually, many people are not leaving their friends. They are going to join them. My wife and I, for example, now know more people who live abroad than we know who live in Britain. Our Christmas cards have to be posted in November.)

Look at any graph showing immigration and emigration figures and you can immediately tell when Brown took over as Chancellor. The graph showing the net immigration figures went up almost vertically when Brown took office in 1997. (And the immigration figures are certain to be much, much higher than the official estimates.) At the same time the number of Britons leaving – and not coming back – started to rise. And the number of Britons leaving has continued to rise ever since.

The inevitable result of this exodus is that Brown and company get safer by the year. (The people who leave are the people who will probably never vote Labour). The downside for Labour (and the rest of the country) is that the people who leave are, generally speaking, hard-working and at least moderately well off. These people are taking their work ethic, their money, their pensions and their ideas out of the country. Britain must inevitably head further and deeper towards recession.

The Government is so committed to spending money on its army of advisers and civil servants (and on voters who receive benefits) that taxes are going to have to rise dramatically. The Labour philosophy of taking from the hard working and giving to the indolent (instead of from the rich to the poor) will continue unchecked. But eventually it will come to a sticky end because it won't be long before there won't be any middle-classes left to squeeze.

Chapter Fourteen

PFI: Perfidious Financial Innovation

'Government is every salesman's dream — an idiot with lots of money.'
CHRIS DILLOW, *INVESTORS CHRONICLE*

Brown warmly embraced the principle of Private Finance Initiative (PFI). Although he didn't invent it, it is one of the things for which he will be best remembered. As a Chancellor with a huge spending problem he found PFI a splendid way to spend, spend, spend without actually having to pay the bills. (He has left the bills to be paid by future generations.)

Under the PFI banner, and Gordon's supervision, the Government, on our behalf, signed more than 750 separate deals with private companies to build, service and maintain all sorts of public sector projects — including schools, hospitals, prisons, roads and defence facilities. (Of the 68 hospitals completed during the first eight years of Brown's Chancellorship, an astonishing 64 were PFI projects.)

Under Brown, PFI became a booming £4 billion a year industry, giving many financiers a steady, dependable income stream and huge profits.

The usual PFI deal is basically quite simple: a private company raises some money, builds a school and finds a team to maintain and service it. The company then effectively leases the school to

90

the Government. Eventually, when the school is crumbling and pretty much worthless, ownership is passed to the State.

By early 2007, PFI had been used to build 230 new schools, 185 new hospitals and health centres and 43 roads and bridges. Under Gordon's 'management' (I use the word ironically) PFI now makes up between 10 and 15% of all public sector investment.

Brown claims that PFI gives the Government greater access to private capital. This, of course, is the usual garbage most people now expect from a man with no experience of business. Brown would have made a useless businessman (I suspect he would have quickly become another bankruptcy statistic) but he would have made a wonderful confidence trickster (especially in partnership with glib, 'trust me' Tony Blair).

In theory, PFI sounds a moderately good idea. It's certainly no worse than most of the ideas that get kicked around by half-witted politicians.

In reality, PFI was loved by Brown because it is just a huge accounting fiddle. A massive, expensive, hire purchase scheme which enabled him to keep infrastructure spending off the Government's current account and shifted the cost onto future Chancellors and future taxpayers. The PFI is a trick Brown uses to keep huge public spending commitments off the public books by claiming that they belong to the private sector.

It was PFI which enabled Brown to keep public borrowing below 40% of gross domestic product (GDP). Gordon used PFI to help maintain his fiction of prudence. Sadly, generations to come will be paying for his vanity, for the reality, of course, is that the firms involved must eventually be paid. The debts the Government has built up in persuading private companies to build schools, roads and hospitals are now estimated to be £55 billion. Many of the bankers who have financed the projects have done absurdly well out of the Government – walking away with massive windfall profits. (One group of city slickers walked away from a PFI deal with a return of 662%.) All this money will have to be found by future taxpayers.

Incidentally, it is usually thought that one of the signs of a fascist society is one where government and business are merged. The Private Finance Initiative is, of course, a perfect, practical example of fascism in action. Everyone wins except the people. Government wins because the politicians can delay the cost of their spending programmes (thereby enabling them to convince the voters that they are managing the economy well) and business wins because the financiers can make a lot of money.

MPs on the Public Accounts Committee (the watchdog responsible for making sure that taxpayers get value for money) put their fingers on the problem by coming to the conclusion that 'civil servants are regularly being outwitted by their commercial, sophisticated private-sector counterparts'.

The trouble, of course, was that Brown and his little friends at the Treasury thought they were bright and could outwit the nasty oiks with £200 haircuts and silk suits. Sadly, not only is Gordon a moron. So, it seems, were most of his little chums.

Right from the beginning the guys with the £200 haircuts and the silk suits were outwitting Gordon and his pathetic little pals. Some made huge one-off profits by finding more favourable loans once their building had been finished. For example, the Public Accounts Committee pointed out that the private investors who built the Norfolk and Norwich Hospital made a cool £80 million by using debt refinancing to increase returns from a decent 16% to a bonus-boosting 60%.

When Brown and his half-wits at the Treasury realised that the boys in silk suits were making far more money than had been envisaged they naturally changed the rules. They persuaded investors to hand back a percentage of any extra profits gained by refinancing.

Naturally, the Government hasn't done anywhere near as well out of this as Brown had expected. The silk suits have once again managed to out-negotiate the civil servants. They are now making even bigger profits by selling equity stakes to additional partners. So, for example, a company called Mowlam invested £3.4 million in the Docklands Light Railway and sold its stake for £19.4 million. The equity in the rebuilding of the M40 motorway has been sold at least five times, with different builders making huge profits. One company sold a prison for six times what it had paid. The silk-suited boys are giving themselves multimillion pound bonuses.

The next generation of taxpayers, and the generation after that, will for years be paying ever higher taxes because of Brown's stupidity.

Not that the problems are all in the future.

Some public sector users have, for some time, been struggling to meet payments due to private owners of public facilities.

Despite the obvious problems, Gordon was so seduced by the slick way PFI enabled him to be careless with other people's money, while still presenting a facade of prudence, that he remained loyal to this disastrous scheme right up until the end of his Chancellorship.

(Gordon's most notable talent – possibly his only one – has always been his ability, shared with his predecessor, of being able to avoid the truth and find ways to wriggle out of responsibility.)

In his 2006 budget, Gordon claimed that 'PFI is delivering'. Indeed, this was true. The problem was that although it was delivering to private companies it wasn't delivering much except massive debts to taxpayers.

By the time Brown tottered next door to take over the job he thought he was entitled to, he had committed future generations to £54 billion worth of buildings. That, at least, is the debt he said he'd lumbered them with and it sounds bad enough. In reality the bill will be closer to £160 billion.

PFI was never a good idea. It was merely an opportunity for Gordon to mortgage the future. The only good thing about it was that PFI projects usually came in under budget and usually came in on time. (Just 20% of PFI projects ran over budget, compared with 73% of projects run directly by civil servants. And just 20% of PFI projects were delivered late, compared with 70% of projects run directly by civil servants. What this shows, of course, is that civil servants are incompetent and very, very stupid.)

Governments (being less likely to go bust) will always be able to borrow money more cheaply than private companies. If Gordon knew anything about finance and government he would know that. By allowing private companies to borrow money on his behalf Brown simply increased the cost to taxpayers.

★ ★ ★

In addition to his enthusiasm for PFI, Brown has also been a fan of Public Private Partnerships (PPP).

It was his support for Metronet, the PPP London tube project, in the face of opposition from the Mayor of London, which resulted in the project going ahead. (Brown was described by the *Financial Times* as the architect of Metronet).

In July 2007, the £17 billion development had to call in an administrator, though at the time no one seemed entirely clear who would pick up the final bill. My original guess was that it would be the taxpayer and I wasn't disappointed. Taxpayers paid the £2 billion cost over-run, the £2.6 debt and the administrator's tax bill. In a just world Brown would have been forced to find the massive shortfall out of his fat salary and pension.

The whole project had been forced through by Gordon Brown four years earlier despite the fact that the deal was apparently seriously flawed.

Why did Brown force through a plan which involved different organisations maintaining the track and running the trains? Trains and stations were staffed with state employees but maintenance was leased out to private contractors. This was always a disaster waiting to happen.

Presumably, at least one reason for Brown's misplaced enthusiasm was the need to take the cost of the project out of the current accounts by persuading public companies to stump up some of the cash in return for plenty of jam later. Notionally the costs and the risk were taken off the Treasury's books. In practice, they weren't of course. Everyone knew that in the final resort the Government would have to pay whatever it cost to keep the tube running.

Here, surely, was yet another example of Brown's poor judgement. The conclusion among financial observers seemed to be that the city had, once again, run rings around the civil servants and, of course, Gordon Brown.

Brown's contempt for taxpayers and investors seems unending. Shriti 'granny' Vadera, a former adviser to Gordon Brown when he was Chancellor, was made a peer and minister when Brown became Prime Minister. 'Granny' Vadera had a major role in the Government's theft of Railtrack from investors. When investors went to court over their losses it was the loathsome Vadera who was revealed to have dismissed shareholders as 'grannies'.

Her other main claim to fame seems to have been her involvement with the London Underground public-private partnership which later collapsed.

She is said to be an expert on the economies of developing countries and considering the amount of damage Brown has done to the British economy any knowledge Gordon's 'granny' has in this area may well prove valuable to Britain in the future.

★ ★ ★

Not all of these partnerships between the Government and private industry start with a clean piece of land and a plan.

Roads and bridges which taxpayers paid for before Brown became Chancellor have been sold to private companies so that taxpayers can be charged fees to use them.

Just in case that isn't clear I'll put it another way.

Things you and I bought and paid for with our taxes are being sold, by people we elected to look after us, to commercial companies so that they can rent them back to us.

And we allow this to happen?

This isn't only happening to roads and bridges, of course.

In a bizarre reversal of the nationalisation policies once so loved by socialists the Labour Government, under the Chancellorship of Gordon Brown, began selling off huge areas of British public life.

The running of public hospitals, schools and other institutions has been auctioned off to private corporations (often foreign based).

This has been done at a furious pace and it has been done to help Gordon Brown balance the national budget.

It is a case of selling off the family silver.

The difference is that Brown has been selling off silver that doesn't belong to him. It's not the rich landowner who is selling off the family silver but the hired estate manager.

Chapter Fifteen
The Tax Collector

'There are now enough tax inspectors in Britain to fill every seat in the Olympic Stadium in Berlin where the World Cup Final was held – and you'd still have 30,000 waiting outside for tickets.'
GEORGE OSBORNE

After ten years with Gordon Brown in charge of the nation's purse strings, the Government now takes 43% of the nation's income.

This is the highest level for decades and is a practical example of the way Brown's statist philosophy has altered the British economy. Statism has, after all, been the hallmark of Brown's Chancellorship.

The personal tax burden more than doubled between 1997 and 2007. Thanks to taxes introduced by Brown, the tax burden will reach 38.1% of national income by 2009/10. It was 34.8% in 2006/7.

The overall effect of Brown's changes in taxes and benefits has been to reduce work incentives, says the Institute for Fiscal Studies. According to the Organisation for Economic Cooperation and Development (OECD) Britain has had one of the biggest surges in long-term sickness claims of any major world economy over the past five years. The bill for supporting incapacity benefit claimants, single parents and the unemployed is now billions of pounds a year. High tax levels, raised to pay for this sort of irresponsible spending, will drag down the economy at a time when Britain will be at her weakest.

Brown has consistently, and presumably deliberately, made tax more complicated. (The more complicated tax legislation is, the easier it is for the authorities to find errors in tax returns.) Tolley's *Yellow Tax Handbook* on direct taxation had 4,555 pages in it for 1996-7 (the year before Gordon Brown became Chancellor of the Exchequer). The edition for 2005-6 had 9,050 pages and it's growing every time Brown opens his mouth. In 2007, Tolley's had reached 9,806 pages. Even professional accountants admit that they can't keep up – and nor can I HM Revenue and Customs' own staff. I have been officially told that the advice offered by Revenue staff is not always to be relied upon. Astonishingly, HM Revenue and Customs now aims for 75%-80% accuracy.

Britain has, under Brown, moved from being a low-tax country to a high tax country. A series of tinkerings and stealth taxes have weakened British industry and sent a good many native high earners offshore in search of less punitive regimes.

It hasn't just been national taxes which have risen massively under Brown.

Council tax bills rose three times faster than (official) inflation and twice as fast as average earnings between 1997 and 2007. Council taxes actually managed to double in a decade. The average council tax bill went up by nearly 40% between 2003 and 2007 – while during the same period services were cut dramatically. All the evidence shows that council taxes will continue to have to rise far faster than inflation, partly because of cuts in central Government expenditure and partly in order to pay pensions for retired council officers. Services will decline and deteriorate.

Brown pledged not to increase income tax. Technically, he didn't. But the tax burden on Britons under his stewardship has risen dramatically. Brown has taken advantage of fiscal creep whereby as inflation pushes up wages so more and more people find themselves pushed into higher tax brackets; he has abolished the lowest tax band (thereby increasing taxes on the poor) and, of course, he has introduced more new, crafty, sneaky taxes than anyone in history.

It was Brown's new tax on landfill that forced many local authorities to scrap weekly rubbish collections. It was his stealth tax on pensions that destroyed pensions for millions. The British now pay 40% inheritance tax on any sum inherited over £300,000, 4% in stamp duty on any property costing more than £500,000, 0.5% stamp duty on shares and tax on capital gains. Sweden and France, both countries which have a long tradition of taxing private wealth to finance their welfare states, have been cutting taxes on capital. Not Gordon Brown. Until he took over in 1997, Britain was leading the world in tax cutting. Now, thanks to Brown, Britain leads the world in tax rises – unless you're foreign or a city slicker specialising in private equity.

Brown's new taxes aren't just sending British entrepreneurs abroad, they are also distorting the economy (people put their money into buying an expensive house rather than building up a business because, when they sell, there is no Capital Gains tax to pay), reducing investment (there is no incentive to make a profit when the tax rates are so high) and destroying private wealth (which people who aren't lucky enough to have a Gordon Brown sized pension will need in order to survive in their pension-damaged old age). Private wealth is what funds small start-up companies. And it is what enables people to survive in old age. Capitalism needs capital. Gordon Brown doesn't understand that. He wants capitalism without private capital. And that is what Mussolini would have probably described as fascism in action.

> The Swiss have far lower tax rates than Britain, enjoy a system of real democracy and yet have an infrastructure system that is a million times better than Britain's. You can set your watch by their trains. (Trains which do not, incidentally, stop running if there is snow falling.)

Gordon the Moron has constantly targeted the middle classes. I don't know whether he does this because he hates people who work hard and have proper jobs (not that I'm convinced that he, or anyone else in his immediate circle, has much idea about what a proper job is, or what it entails) or just because the middle classes, being polite, busy and more likely than most to bow down to authority, tend to pay up without too much of a fuss. Possibly both. And, as I illustrate quite vividly elsewhere in this book, he seems to like targeting the English in a way that might, I suspect, be considered racist if the Scots were the target.

★ ★ ★

While Gordon Brown was in charge of the nation's finances British motorists paid £50 billion a year to their Government. But the Government spent £10 billion a year on providing roads for them to drive on. After ten years with Gordon Brown controlling the purse strings, Britain has a quarter of the main roads per million cars as has France and half as many as the European average.

During Gordon Brown's reign as Chancellor of the Exchequer the number of speed cameras in Britain has, however, increased dramatically. It is widely accepted that these cameras are there simply to raise money for the Government.

A Department of Transport audit of 6,000 speed cameras in England and Wales in 2004 found that the number of people killed or seriously injured had gone up at one in seven camera sites. At 743 camera locations the number of deaths or serious casualties had increased by up to 9%. A second study, conducted by the publication *Motorcycle News*, showed that fatal road accidents have risen dramatically in areas where the use of speed cameras has increased. In Hertfordshire, the number of cameras went up by 24% and the number of road deaths went up by 34.2%. In County Durham, which has just one mobile camera unit, the number of deaths fell by 24%.

The West Midlands Police force dismantled ten speed cameras and removed film from another 50 after admitting that speed cameras could make roads more dangerous. Two of the cameras were obscured by a bridge. One was hidden behind a road sign. The West Midlands Casualty Reduction Partnership (who thinks up these names?) admitted that motorists had been braking suddenly after spotting the cameras at the last minute and that there was 'a potential safety hazard'. Other research has suggested that speed cameras create more accidents because motorists and motorcyclists accelerate away from the cameras too quickly. There have also been suggestions that motorists avoid fixed camera sites by taking other (often more congested, potentially more dangerous, routes). And throughout the country in recent years, despite the spread of speed cameras, the figures show that the number of road deaths has increased steadily.

Naturally, the Labour Party has ignored the facts and has claimed that accidents are going down and speed cameras are saving lives.

The repeated suppression of the truth about speed cameras shows that the Government has for years been ruthlessly committed to making money rather than saving lives. Speeding fines are, quite simply, another form of taxation.

It's difficult to avoid the conclusion that Government Ministers, well-paid to look after us, have been exploiting us and deliberately endangering our health. And if that's not criminal behaviour I don't know what is.

The Government even wants motorists to pay £600 for a black box so that every driver's movements can be tracked by satellite. After ten years of a hailstorm of rules, regulations and taxes the Government estimates that there are now two million people in Britain driving cars which are unlicensed and uninsured. What a surprise.

★ ★ ★

When Gordon Brown complained about the rising price of oil he pointed out, with the sort of breathtaking hypocrisy which is now widely associated with the Labour Party, that the high cost of oil is a tremendous burden on poorer people. Neither he nor any media commentators made any reference to the fact that in the UK 80% of the cost of a gallon of petrol goes direct to the Chancellor of the Exchequer as tax. Britain has the most expensive petrol in the world because the British people pay more fuel tax than anyone else.

Brown has himself made things considerably worse by slapping an extra tax on oil companies.

The Labour Government is either too stupid to realise, or simply doesn't care, that a windfall tax on oil companies will discourage them from investing in further exploration and will therefore hasten the arrival of the point at which the supply of oil is exceeded by the demand.

> The tax burdens in most countries fell between 2001 and 2006 but in the UK, in that period, they rose dramatically. British workers are now the most expensive to employ in the world.

During 2006, over 200,000 Britons reported their friends, neighbours and workmates to HM Revenue and Customs.

The authorities encourage this large scale 'snitching' by offering bribes to citizens who are prepared to suggest suitable candidates for investigation by the authorities. Those reporting their friends, neighbours and workmates do not need to have any evidence. A phone call from a jealous acquaintance reporting that you have just bought a new car or been on holiday will trigger an investigation. Under Gordon Brown, the Treasury has encouraged citizens to spy and snoop on one another. After the Government set up its confidential hotline in 2006, inviting people to inform on friends, colleagues and family to the taxman, thousands took advantage of the opportunity to get someone into trouble.

What sort of world are we living in where people are encouraged to call up the Revenue or Customs offices to report (quite probably without any evidence) that a friend or a member of their family might possibly be fiddling their taxes? Is this all part of a plan to persuade us to put the State before family and friends? Where will Brown put the Gulag?

Taxpayers now often find themselves being told that in order to avoid huge tax penalties they must prove a negative. ('Prove that you didn't earn an undeclared £1,000,000 and hide it somewhere. If you don't do this we will hit you with a massive tax demand.'). It is, of course, impossible to prove a negative.

Tax should be more than a punishment or an obligation. It is a duty which honest citizens pay as the membership fee for the society in which they live. But, through a mixture of deviousness, crookedness and bullying the Government has created enmity and distrust between honest taxpayers and the Government. Gordon Brown seems to assume that all money belongs to the State and that anyone who has money of their own must have stolen it from the State. This view seems to have spread down through the

Government and into all branches of the civil service – particularly the branch which collects taxes.

Tax collecting long ago became politically motivated extortion. Some tax collecting schemes don't even make a profit and can only be described as punitive and vindictive. For example, Capital Gains Tax costs more to collect than it produces. It is therefore merely vindictive.

Today, more and more people regard tax as protection money; a brutal necessity, part of staying alive and being in business. Taxpayers hand over whatever the thugs demand, not because it is honestly owed but because they have no choice. The demand is backed up with a threat of force. Hand over your money or we will come round, smash down your door and drag you away. We pay tax in the same way that shop and restaurant owners pay protection money – so that they don't send people round to break our windows, hurt us or harm us in some way.

According to a report commissioned by the Inland Revenue, small companies bear 80% of the burden of red tape in Britain. The average 'small' businessman spends 28 hours a month filling in tax forms of one sort or another. On top of that there is the annual tax form (taking around a week to fill in) and the ensuing (sometimes seemingly endless) enquiries. Plus there is the red tape and bureaucratic interference from other Government departments. And the Government-inspired bureaucracy from banks and insurance companies.

According to official figures people running small businesses now spend a minimum of 25% of their working time on tax, VAT and red tape administration. Many waste much more of their time this way. (Those who don't invariably end up in trouble with the authorities.)

So, over a quarter of the nation's productive time is wasted, by the nation's most productive people. It is this endless official paperwork which is largely responsible for the fact that bankruptcies are rising at a phenomenal rate.

★ ★ ★

In November 2006, the HM Revenue and Customs were still sending out routine letters to people whose payments or credits in any one year were insufficient to count towards the basic state pension, and inviting them to make up the shortfall. These letters were sent out despite the fact that the authorities knew that thousands of people would see no gain at all from paying extra voluntary contributions to their basic state pensions because of changes being brought in by the Government in 2010. If a private company did this the directors would doubtless be arrested for fraud. When the Government commits fraud they get away with it.

★ ★ ★

Here's a list of some of the tax cock-ups which took place while Gordon the Moron was employed as Chancellor of the Exchequer. These are, of course, just the ones to which the Government has admitted. There were undoubtedly many, many more.

1. The on-line system for self-assessment had to be taken off-line for a month after taxpayers found that they could see the tax affairs of other citizens.

2. Hundreds of HM Revenue and Customs documents – including personal tax returns – were dumped at the side of a road in Nottingham in the spring of 2007.

3. One in four tax returns was processed wrongly in 2002.

4. In 2002, the Inland Revenue sold its own buildings in London to a company based in a tax haven.

5. In 2003, the Inland Revenue failed to make prompt payments of tax credits and caused a political crisis.

6. About five million individual taxpayers received their tax returns up to a month late, holding up payment of millions of pounds in refunds. Her Majesty's Revenue and Customs blamed the delay on 'production issues'.

7. In 2003, the Treasury issued a 12-page briefing note to senior officials working at the Treasury, explaining how they could lighten their personal tax burden through tax avoidance techniques. The head of tax at a major accounting firm was so impressed with the tax avoidance advice offered by the Treasury to its own civil servants that he is alleged to have offered a job to the civil servant who prepared the briefing.

8. Tax in Britain is so complex that when an American banker was hired by Lloyds Bank, her salary included £25,000 a year to pay for tax advice.

9. On a single day, I received three envelopes from the Inland Revenue. The three envelopes each contained pieces of paper giving me an up-to-date account of my tax affairs. I've read instructions for Chinese DVD players which made more sense. The three forms I'd been sent all contained different assessments. The best (from my point of view) informed me that the Government owed me around £600. The worst said I owed them around £300. Confused, I telephoned to find out which was accurate. The Inland Revenue employee to whom I spoke told me that the Government owed me £9,833.71. I said I liked that assessment best and would accept it and throw the other three away.

10. The National Audit Office has published a report stating that confusion over the collection of income tax through PAYE had affected six million taxpayers in 2006. Taxpayers are reputed to have overpaid £500 million but Revenue and Customs were generously offering not to repay any of this money. On the other hand, Revenue and Customs was also owed £1 billion that hadn't been paid and which wouldn't be pursued. The National Audit Office also found that in 2003/4 the Revenue had stated that it paid tax credits of between £1.06 billion and £1.28 billion to claimants who were not entitled to them. The head of the HMRC admitted to a committee of taxpayers that roughly a third of all PAYE taxpayers were either paying too much tax or else paying too little tax. The words 'shambles' and 'incompetence' keep coming into my mind but I cannot imagine why.

11. The Government insists that we keep vast quantities of paperwork, going back many years, if we wish to defend ourselves against frivolous and outrageous accusations from HM Revenue and Customs. Every piece of paper that we are forced to keep increases the risk of identity theft. And the Government insists that preventing identity theft is vital in the fight against terrorism.

12. Rightmove, the Internet estate agent, will be paid £10

million of taxpayers' money to pass all its data about 800,000 English properties to the UK Government's Valuation Office Agency. This will give the taxman access to information about every home advertised on the property web site since it was launched seven years ago. Six out of ten estate agents put their properties on Rightmove. House sellers and house buyers were not told that their information would be passed on to the Government. The Government will use the information to decide how much council tax must be paid on a home. They will, inevitably, try to use the information to raise taxes. (They are clearly hoping to make a profit on their £10,000,000 investment.)

13. MPs in general claimed an average of £17,852 a year in 2005 for the cost of keeping houses in their constituencies. Gordon Brown claimed more than average. He claimed £18,681 to run his second home.

14. HM Revenue and Customs has, for many years, demanded interest if payments owed to them are paid late. They are now planning to take anything they think they are owed direct from taxpayers' bank accounts. It is, you will be surprised to learn, different if HM Revenue and Customs owe money to taxpayers. For one thing, the interest rate they pay when they owe money is lower than the interest rate they charge if you owe them money. And for another you may well find yourself waiting a long time for your repayment.

★ ★ ★

I strongly suspect that tax investigations actually lose the country money. In other words, I suspect that the amount of money the tax people collect after chasing taxpayers is exceeded by the amount lost because small companies and individuals stop productive work to deal with paperwork from the HM Revenue and Customs. And how many innocent taxpayers, fed up with being harassed, give up, retire or emigrate? Tax investigations are like tax rates; above a certain level of annoyance they result in lower earnings for the State; tax collecting becomes counter-productive and rather than increasing the tax take is a huge drain on the nation.

★ ★ ★

The tax authorities have always been high-handed and illogical. P.G.Wodehouse got so fed up with their nonsense that he famously wrote 'you simply hit them with an axe'. George Orwell became so frustrated and enraged that he threw letters from the taxman into the bin unopened. How, I wonder, would they cope with today's nonsense?

★ ★ ★

The principle of ignorance of the law is acceptable when laws are logical and easy to understand. (Don't murder, don't steal, etc.). But when the laws are incomprehensible, confusing and contradictory (and constantly altered prospectively and retrospectively), and when even the experts in a particular area can't keep up with the laws then the principle becomes unreasonable and contrary to good sense and to basic human rights.

'Taxes are the price we pay for a civilised society,' said Oliver Wendell Holmes. And he was right. But uncivilised tax enquiries are too high a price and they threaten the fabric of our society. Government employees have created a world in which the divisions between the State and its functionaries, on the one hand, and the citizens (and their families) on the other, grow wider by the day. There is growing distrust and disappointment and anger and resentment among people who create the wealth which pays for the State. Without the support of taxpayers there will be no money and, therefore, no State and no comfy jobs for the functionaries. Today, tax collectors bully and frighten taxpayers into giving in and paying money they don't owe in just the same sort of intrinsically dishonest way that insurance companies avoid their financial responsibilities when a policyholder attempts to make a legitimate claim. Both claim, unfairly, that their aggressive tactics are justified by the dishonest activities of a minority. If the existence of violence and deceit is used as an excuse for violence and deceit then where is our civilisation?

★ ★ ★

There are still some innocents left who believe that only the guilty are ever targeted by the tax authorities. 'If you haven't done anything wrong then you have nothing to fear,' is their cry. The truth is that, in its constant search for extra money, HM Revenue and Customs now regularly targets taxpayers chosen on a random basis. Routine, random enquiries enable tax inspectors to delve into every area of a taxpayer's life. Such routine enquiries often last between 12 and 18 months. Those innocents who survive such enquiries are, by the end, invariably drained and utterly exhausted. Those who are self-employed, and who are unable to work because of the depth and extent of the enquiry, may be ruined by the experience – however innocent they may be. Innocence and honesty are no longer a defence.

> The average family now pays £1,300 more tax per year than when Brown took office. Despite this the Government now needs to make severe spending cuts and to raise another £20 billion in the next five years to have any hope of making the budget balance.

During Gordon Brown's decade in charge of the nation's finances, a growing number of British companies have been sold to foreign owners. In 2006 alone, foreign companies spent £75.5 billion buying famous British companies. Back in 1996, the year before Brown became Chancellor, the figure was £9 billion.

So far nearly 500 British companies have been sold to foreign owners. The list includes many basic infrastructure companies such as those providing water supplies. Not only does this mean that these companies are run without any thought for the needs of the British people but it also means that jobs and priorities will be out-sourced to other countries. And, of course, foreign-owned companies tend to make decisions in their own national interests rather than in Britain's interests.

Gordon Brown may not yet have realised this but many of these companies are set up abroad and pay tax abroad. If your head office is in Bermuda or Dublin where tax rates are much lower you can avoid British taxes.

One trick popular among foreign buyers of British companies is to load up the acquired British business with debt. Then, what used to be profit goes to paying off the debt so there is no profit on which to pay tax in Britain.

Naturally, as the number of British owned companies falls so the tax burden on companies remaining in the UK goes up. The end result is that British companies either get weak (and also bought) or go bust. (The National Audit Office has found that one-third of the UK's biggest businesses are paying no corporation tax and almost another third are paying £10, or less, a year.)

Alternatively, companies simply arrange to allocate their costs and adjust their pricing so that very little tax is paid in Britain. So, for example, the profit margin of one big international company in the UK was recently quoted as just 3.2%. The group's worldwide profit margin was 18.4%.

Additionally, foreigners now own 40% of the British stock market – up from 28% in 1997. This is more than is held by British individuals, British pension funds and British investment and unit trusts put together. By 2006, British individuals directly owned only 12.8% of UK equities – that's a smaller portion than ever before. All this means that the dividends paid by those companies go abroad.

★ ★ ★

Gordon Brown thinks Scotsman Adam Smith was a great thinker, and Smith now appears on England's new £20 note. But read what Smith had to say about tax in his seminal work *The Nature and Causes Of The Wealth Of Nations:*

'Every tax ought to be so contrived as both to take out and to keep out of the pockets of the people as little as possible, over and above what it brings into the public treasury of the state. A tax may either take out or keep out of the pockets of the people a great deal more than it brings into the public treasury in the four following ways. First, the levying of it may require a great number of officers, whose salaries may eat up the greater part of the produce of the tax, and those perquisites may impose another additional tax upon the people. Secondly, it may obstruct the industry of the people, and discourage them from applying to certain branches of business which might give maintenance and employment to great multitudes. While it obliges the people to pay, it may thus diminish, or perhaps destroy some of the funds, which might enable them more easily to do so. Thirdly, by the forfeitures and other penalties which those unfortunate individuals incur who attempt unsuccessfully to evade the tax, it may frequently ruin them, and thereby put an end to the benefit from which the community might have received from the employment of their capitals. Fourthly, by subjecting the people to the frequent visits, and the odious examination of the tax-gatherers, it may expose them to much unnecessary trouble, vexation, and oppression; and though vexation is not, strictly speaking, expense, it is certainly equivalent to the expense at which every man would be willing to redeem himself from it. It is in some one or other of these four different ways that taxes are frequently so much burdensome to the people than they are beneficial to the sovereign.'

Chapter Sixteen
Means-Testing – Another Aspect Of Practical Fascism

'If I spend somebody else's money on somebody else, I'm not concerned about how much it is, and I'm not concerned about what I get. And that's government.'
MILTON FRIEDMAN

Gordon Brown is an enthusiastic supporter of means-testing – one of the worst and most invidious aspects of the variety of modern fascism he seems to me to espouse. The principle (if you can call it that) is that people who work hard and earn more should be denied help by the State while the feckless, who have spent whatever money they may have had, should be supported by the State. The Government has even introduced a rising scale of punishments for citizens so that those who work hard and earn more may be forced to pay greater fines than those who do not work at all.

Means-testing is, of course, always illogical, unfair and unjust.

Someone who has paid tax has already contributed to society. Why should he or she be denied the help offered freely to people who haven't contributed anything to society?

In Brown's new world of means-testing the less money you save the more you will be given. The poorer you are the more likely you are to receive everything free. If you are poor and you spend everything the State has given you then your debts will be paid. In Brown's world there is no point at all in saving. In Brown's world the wise virgin does not save her oil – she burns it, knowing that the authorities will take from those who save and share their oil with her. In Gordon Brown's world the poor get everything free – as long as they are prepared to allow the State to control their lives. In his world, the new non-working poor are the new rich.

Brown is probably not bright enough to realise it, but he has destroyed the point of saving and has encouraged new generations to spend, spend, spend in the expectation that the State will look after them. Only the foolish save in the world Gordon Brown has created.

For means-testing to be fair, the Government would have to take into consideration the special needs of those who work. So, for example, business people hurrying to appointments would be given priority in traffic or when looking for parking places. There would be special queues in Post Offices for business people needing postal services, rather than handouts from the State. And the NHS would provide priority healthcare for those who need to be fit in order to work (and pay tax). If means-testing is to be fair, then it has to operate both ways.

Chapter Seventeen

An Army Of Bureaucrats

*'Governments and their civil servants are in a different league.
When they pull a fast one, the scale of their underhand dealing
is breathtaking.'*
CLIVE EGLETON, *THE HONEY TRAP*

Keeping interest rates artificially low enabled Brown to issue a flood of 50-year Government bonds at a record low cost. It was this cheap money that enabled the Government to spend spend spend on hiring new staff. The Government has, in fact, been hiring its way out of bad unemployment figures (turning all those unemployed people into underemployed civil servants).

The problem will come when the Government can no longer borrow money quite as easily. Who, then, will pay the salaries and pensions for all those new, unnecessary employees? I suspect that Gordon doesn't care. He will, by then, be enjoying his massive pension – paid for by English taxpayers.

Under Brown, the number of people employed in the public sector grew by 900,000. By summer 2007, the State was directly employing seven million people. That's 24% of the entire workforce. One in four Britons now work for the Government or for local councils – and many spend much or most of their time finding ways to prevent the three out of four who are in productive employment from working efficiently and effectively.

112

A massive 37% of the increase in employment that has taken place during Brown's chancellorship has been in the public sector. And what a glorious time it has been to be a civil servant. Public sector employees now earn more money than private sector employees, they have uninterrupted weekends and work shorter hours, have far more generous pensions (which they can take considerably earlier), have longer holidays and have the sort of job security that would have been envied in Japan half a century ago.

National and local Government employees are the new aristocracy. They enjoy short, flexible working hours, virtually guaranteed lifetime employment (whatever they do wrong), a total lack of personal responsibility and immunity to the vagaries of the market.

The rise in the number of public employees cannot be blamed on the rising population because the number of people employed by the Government is actually going up faster than the population. So, for example, in the north west of England the overall population has risen by 54,000 since 1999 but in the same period the public sector has taken on 83,000 new workers. It makes no sort of sense to employ another 83,000 workers to cope with the extra work produced by servicing the needs of an extra 54,000 citizens.

I suspect that the Government's plan was always to get more than 50% of the voters on its payroll (Actually they need less than that, of course, since only around 70% of the population bother to vote.)

By increasing the Government payroll, and by dramatically increasing the number of people on benefits, Brown has been able to ensure that he (and his party) can stay in power for years to come.

★ ★ ★

In Brown's world, public employment has been divorced from public responsibility. If a private sector individual such as a doctor or a shopkeeper makes a mistake he or she must pay for the error. They will be forced to pay in many ways. Often they will be financially ruined. But public service employees get away scot- free and are allowed to repeat their mistakes endlessly and anonymously while the public just goes on paying. Time and time again public employees are found guilty of gross incompetence but aren't sacked. They aren't even fined. They receive no disciplinary action. If, for example, a hospital employee does something wrong it is their employer (the hospital) which is fined. So public money is used and the public suffers because there is less money left to pay for running the hospital. Complaints procedures for those wishing to complain about Government employees invariably end up persecuting the complainant rather than the offending employee – whom the system is designed to protect.

As anyone who has ever tried to complain about a Government employee will know, Government employees are, in practice, immune to criticism and can make whatever errors they like without fear of chastisement or dismissal.

A proposed new law, the Corporate Manslaughter Act, was designed to put company directors in the dock if they were considered to be responsible for any deaths. But the law was specifically designed not to apply to State-owned facilities such as prisons or social service departments so that public sector workers would be immune. Ministers were worried that the burden of responsibility would be too much for civil servants to bear.

State employees (and those on benefits) are having it good. These are the very best years to be a Government employee. But, sadly for them, the best years will not last long. The country is running out of money and Brown's cohorts are heading for a very sticky end.

★ ★ ★

Before Gordon Brown took over at the Treasury, the State sector consumed 37% of Britain's Gross Domestic Product (GDP) and the economy was in an impressively healthy state. ('What am I supposed to do, send a note of thanks?' Gordon is reported to have asked, in a rare flash of what his supporters might describe as wit, when he took office and was told by civil servants that the economy was in a healthy state.) After ten years with Brown in charge, the State sector's share of GDP had risen to 45%.

When Gordon left his job as Chancellor to become Prime Minister his efforts had produced a budget deficit of 3% at the top of the economic cycle. He left a current account deficit of 3.4% of GDP.

Brown's approach to the public sector is comparable to that of Stalin. His administration is as inefficient as Stalin's too. Under Brown's management of the economy, strikes by civil servants have rocketed. In 2006, there were around 150 public sector stoppages and 650,000 working days were lost. That's a massive increase on previous years. It's five times as many as there were in 2005, and more than there were in 2004 and 2005 together. Amazingly, many of these disputes were triggered by civil servants complaining about their working conditions. (Conditions which are invariably better in every respect than working conditions in the private sector.)

A report from the Institute of Economic Affairs concluded that if civil servants in Britain were as efficient as their Japanese, American or Australian counterparts a staggering £80 billion could be handed back to taxpayers every year.

State employees have been allowed to work shorter hours and to choose their working hours without regard for the needs of the consumer – the taxpayer – and productivity by state employees has dropped alarmingly as a result.

Creating high paying jobs in the public sector has helped encourage the creation of an army of people (many of whom earn over £100,000 a year) who have a vested interest in extending their departments, hiring assistants and building empires. Hospital administrators, for example, now often earn more than doctors and it is they, not the doctors, who make the decisions which decide how hospitals should be run.

The bureaucrats, the administrators, the creators of red tape, contribute little or nothing to society. On the contrary, their work is often designed to make life ever more difficult for those who are trying to contribute to society – by creating businesses and jobs.

Gordon Brown has presided over the biggest ever expansion of the State.

And it's no accident.

Because Gordon Brown is a statist.

And he knows that people who get their bread from the Government are likely to be loyal to it.

Chapter Eighteen

A Man Dedicated To Waste

*'I did maths for a year at university. I don't think I was very good at
it. And some people would say it shows.'*
GORDON BROWN

Vast amounts of money were wasted during Gordon's tenure as
Chancellor of the Exchequer. Here are just a few examples:

1. Between £2 billion and £3 billion a year has been wasted
    on advisers and consultants during Brown's years as Chancellor
    of the Exchequer. Providing consultancy services for the
    Government has, under Brown, become a bran tub extravaganza
    for charlatans and swindlers. Consultants charge £2,000 a day
    for services such as advising how to buy a new computer system,
    how to carry out a survey and how to manage change. HM
    Revenue and Customs spent £106 million on management
    consultants in 2006 in an attempt to save money. As a result
    they saved £105 million by cutting staff. Numerous companies
    and individuals have made a fortune out of providing advice
    for the Government. MPs who looked into the habit of hiring
    outside advice found that four out of ten public sector bosses
    admitted that they had hired consultants unnecessarily. Many
    admitted that they didn't know how much they had spent or
    if the benefits justified the costs.

2. More than 5,000 civil servants at the Home Office shared bonus payments totalling £3.6 million of taxpayers' money in 2006. In the year that these payments were made the Home Secretary, John Reid, declared that the Home Office department was 'not fit for purpose' after it was revealed that more than 1,000 foreign criminals had been released from prison without being considered for deportation. The Home Office made a number of other blunders. Despite their bungling of the payments system which caused severe financial hardship to farmers, civil servants were paid £572,000 in performance-related bonuses. Just before the First World War the Home Office employed 28 people. Today, the Home Office employs 70,000 people. What on earth do all those people actually do? It is, perhaps, hardly surprising that such a bloated department should be so grotesquely inefficient and have such a reputation for institutionalised incompetence.

3. While British soldiers in Iraq were forced to borrow equipment from one another, and to purchase necessary items out of their own meagre wages, the top brass were allowed to spend vast amounts of taxpayers' money on servants – including valets, gardeners and chefs. While the Government closed down specialist military hospitals to save money, senior army chiefs were allowed to have up to six servants each. A father of one soldier who was killed pointed out that his son had not been given a distress flare costing £1.50 and was, therefore, not able to signal for help when he was attacked. Meanwhile, Brown allowed taxpayers' money to be spent on hiring people to fold napkins, polish cutlery and water the plants for army generals.

4. Between March 2004 and March 2007, the head of the National Audit Office (NAO), the man employed by the Government to ensure that public money is spent properly, made 43 trips abroad (accompanied by his wife on 22 of them) at a cost of £336,000. In 2005 alone, the head of the NAO, Sir John Bourn made 15 trips to universally interesting places. He travelled first class on long journeys and slummed it in business class on short trips. He and Lady Bourn enjoyed numerous

stays in five star hotels at taxpayers' expense. Places visited included the Bahamas, Paris, Rome, Geneva, Mauritius, New York, Brazil, Berne and Auckland (New Zealand). 'I can't see why the Auditor General needs to go abroad at all,' said one MP. 'One would expect someone in his position to set an example.' A former parliamentary watchdog, removed from his job (perhaps for barking and biting too much), criticised Sir John's role for being little more than that of Prime Minister's poodle. Looking at Sir John's itinerary it seems to me that the head of the National Audit Office came home only to pick up another case full of clean shirts. In three years, he spent 1,068 days abroad. Maybe if he'd stayed at home a little more the National Audit Office would have done more to stop Gordon Brown wasting so much taxpayers' money. On the other hand, perhaps Gordon was happy to see the head of the National Audit Office wandering around the world.

5. The Government agency specifically created to seize the assets of criminals, the Assets Recovery Agency, spent £65 million collecting £23 million. The Government responded to this failure by suggesting that the police and other agencies should be allowed to seize high value goods as soon as a suspect was charged, instead of having to wait for a conviction. Ministers also suggested that neighbours could receive huge cash rewards for informing on neighbours who might be living on the proceeds of crime. (The Labour Government has, generally speaking, been very keen on encouraging citizens to inform on relatives, friends, neighbours and customers who they consider might be tax cheats or terrorists or failing to sort their rubbish properly. Breaking down community and family bonds is, of course, a good way for a Government to acquire more power over its citizens.)

6. Staff at the Child Support Agency (CSA) were given £25 million in bonuses in the last five years of the agency's existence, even though the CSA had to be scrapped for failing so badly. (The CSA was responsible for collecting child maintenance payments but had failed to collect £3.5 billion from absent fathers). Staff were paid nearly £4 million

in bonuses in 2006, the year when the Government finally announced that the CSA was going to be scrapped for being totally incompetent.

7. Evidence that civil servants don't work as hard as other people isn't difficult to find. After ten years of Gordon Brown at the Treasury, civil servants were found to be taking 9.1 sick days a year compared to the 6.4 days a year being taken by workers in the private sector. Although civil servants have traditionally enjoyed rather stress-free jobs, many civil servants claimed that they needed to take time off because of the stress of meeting Brownian targets.

8. After the floods which devastated so much of England in the summer of 2007, the Environmental Agency gave huge, five figure bonuses to its senior staff for their work in providing defences against flooding. The flooding in 2007 was widely reported to have been the worst ever seen in England. The publication of the Environmental Agency report which contained details of the bonuses was delayed due to the floods. The National Audit Office had previously criticised the Environmental Agency for failing to keep flood defences in high risk areas up to scratch.

9. When Gordon Brown took over as Chancellor of the Exchequer, Britain was spending £24.1 billion a year on quangos. Ten years later Britain's annual quango bill had risen to £167.5 billion. Many of the 883 quangos British taxpayers now fund are of extremely doubtful value. For example, the Milk Development Council (which spreads the extremely questionable claim that milk is healthy and we should drink more of it) is now reported to employs eight times as many people as it did when New Labour came to power. As a doctor I would argue that the nation would be considerably healthier if the Milk Development Council was closed down completely.

10. If you want to envisage Government waste, remember the photographs of John Prescott playing croquet. Nothing summed up the world of New Labour better than one picture of Prescott with a mallet in his hand.

Chapter Nineteen
A Scot Who Loathes England?

*'He (Gordon Brown) has proved himself to be unintelligent
and obtuse, a natural big government man and a slave to
complexity and obfuscation...'*
ROBIN ANGUS, PERSONAL ASSETS TRUST PLC

Gordon Brown is very much a Scot. A recent major survey showed
that 25% of adults agree that Gordon Brown is 'a Scot who doesn't
understand England'. The evidence suggests that Brown doesn't
care much about England either. Now that Scotland has its own
Parliament it is, of course, appalling that a Scot should be Prime
Minister and responsible for what happens to England and the
English. Brown represents a Scottish constituency and should, if
he wishes to be in politics, be sitting in the Scottish parliament,
making decisions which affect the Scottish. For a decade, Brown
presided over and approved a scandalously unfair system whereby
hard-working English taxpayers supported and subsidised Scottish
citizens (the vast majority of whom received more from the
Government than they paid in tax).

To an outside observer it seems as though Gordon must wake
up in the morning planning a day of stuffing it to the English.

For example, in the summer of 2007, it was revealed that in his
final budget as Chancellor of the Exchequer Brown had (in the

words of the *Financial Times*) 'quietly slashed by a third this year's hospital building and equipment budget in one of his last acts as Chancellor. Prompted by the tightness of the public finances, the new Prime Minister, who has placed the NHS as his 'immediate priority', cut the capital budget of the English NHS for 2007/8 from £6.2 billion to £4.2 billion. The move could delay the Government's hospital building and reconfiguration programme in England. However, Mr Brown avoided equivalent cuts to the Scottish and Welsh NHS budgets even though the funding formula for the UK suggests they should have shared the pain. That decision leaves him open to criticism that he favoured patients in his home country.'

Other media ignored the story which seemed to me to exhibit clear discrimination against those living in England and to provide yet another example of English patients being denied the sort of basic hope and dignity made available to patients in Scotland (at the expense of English taxpayers).

★ ★ ★

Astonishingly, the British Government currently spends between £1,500 and £2,000 more per head on Scottish citizens than it spends on English citizens – resulting in an absurdly generous annual subsidy of £22 billion a year.

It is because of this massive subsidy that Scottish cancer patients are given life-saving drugs which are denied to English patients. It is why English university students must pay their tuition fees while Scottish students get their education free (even if they are studying at an English university). It is why the elderly in England must sell their homes to pay for nursing home care while the elderly in Scotland get free nursing home care. (Very few people in England yet realise how onerous nursing home care can be. A major survey showed that 55% of 45-65 year olds think that the basic state pension of less than £90 a week would cover the cost of their nursing care should they require it, even though the average weekly minimum fee for residential care homes is over £400 a week.) It is why 400,000 elderly people in England are being denied help with dressing, washing and preparing meals, while elderly people in Scotland (where Gordon Brown comes from, remember) receive all these services entirely free of charge. It is why there are free eye tests and free prescriptions for far more patients in Scotland than there are in England.

> Scotland has a population of around five million. Of these only 163,000 are net taxpayers. In other words, of the five million Scots, an astonishing 4,837,000 are kept by English taxpayers.

In Scotland, the State is responsible for 58% of all spending. Indeed, Scotland has one of the highest levels of public expenditure in the Organisation for Economic Cooperation and Development (OECD). Government spending in Scotland is 16% above the UK average.

If Scotland were ever to go it alone, and become truly independent, the Scottish people would have to put up with huge cuts in public spending and services. The North Sea Oil revenues, which Scottish nationalists frequently talk about with exaggerated reverence, would go nowhere near paying for the luxurious Scottish way of life.

Lots of people don't understand why England should be ruled by a Scottish Prime Minister who is allowed to pass laws which affect the English but which don't affect him or his fellow countrymen and who, on being made Prime Minister quickly appointed another Scotsman as Chancellor of the Exchequer. No other country on the planet would be so laid back, so polite and so self-effacing as the English have been in allowing this to happen, especially when you consider that without having to support Scotland, Wales and Northern Ireland, England would have the best public services and the lowest tax rates in the world.

The list of perks given to the Scots (and paid for by the English taxpayers) during Brown's tenure would have embarrassed a more sensitive man.

1. All students in Scotland will get free tuition fees from 2009 whereas students in England and Wales have to pay for their studies themselves. The average degree course now costs £42,000 – leaving students with massive loans to pay off after they have graduated. Students who undertake longer courses

(to study medicine, for example, must pay considerably more). As a result of this gross unfairness more than 37% of pupils in Scotland go to college or university, compared with just 25% of English students. And, remember, it is English taxpayers who are paying for Scottish students to get free university education.

2. Whereas English patients are denied access to expensive new drugs (including vital drugs for the treatment of cancer, Alzheimer's disease and conditions which cause blindness) these drugs are made available to Scottish patients. English taxpayers pay for the drugs given to Scottish patients but are not allowed to have the drugs themselves. Age related macular degeneration is the leading cause of blindness in the UK. It can lead to blindness in as little as three months. There is a drug available which will treat the condition, and therefore prevent blindness, but English patients are frequently refused it on the grounds of cost. A couple in Wiltshire, both of whom had the disease, were told to choose which of them should be treated because their local branch of the NHS told them it could afford to pay for only one. An 84-year-old war veteran, blind in one eye, and losing the sight in the other, was told that he did not merit treatment because he was not an 'exceptional case'. His wife had suffered two broken hips and was entirely dependent on him to look after her.

3. In Scotland, thanks to the English, pensioners get free bus travel and teenagers have discounted bus and train travel.

4. English taxpayers pay for Scottish pensioners to have free central heating installation and free double-glazing. These perks are not available to English pensioners and, as a result, over a million pensioners say they cannot afford their heating bills. Every winter thousands of English pensioners die of the cold.

5. In Scotland, the elderly receive free personal care. If they need help with feeding, dressing and washing they receive it free of charge. If they need to go into a nursing home this is free. They do not have to sell their homes to fund their care. English taxpayers provide the funds for these perks but, in England,

the elderly do not receive free care. On the contrary, they must sell their homes and use up their savings if they need to be looked after in a nursing home.

6. Nurses and other public sector workers receive higher salaries in Scotland than in England. These higher salaries are paid for by English taxpayers.

7. Scottish MPs, voted in by Scottish electors, can vote on issues which affect only England and the English but English MPs have no right to vote on issues which affect the Scots.

8. The Scots are, at a huge cost to English taxpayers, going to be given free prescriptions. The English will still have to pay for their prescriptions.

9. Infant school class sizes in Scotland are to be cut to 18 (with the help of English taxpayers). In England, pupils continue to be taught in classes of 30 or more.

10. Brown has increased stamp duty on houses in the comfortable knowledge that the new rates have little impact on Scotland where the average house is so cheap that there is no stamp duty to pay at all and where, as a result, the much hated inheritance tax is also largely an irrelevance.

Chapter Twenty
A Collapse In Savings

'Getting and spending, we lay waste our powers.'
WILLIAM WORDSWORTH

Thanks to Gordon Brown, the UK saving rate has been negative for the last four years. In other words, for the final four years of Gordon's Chancellorship the average person in the UK spent more than they earned. They borrowed money on their credit cards. They dug into what savings they had. And they borrowed against their houses. In 1997 – before Brown became Chancellor – the British people saved 9.7% of their income. Under Gordon Brown, savings rates in Britain have become the worst since records began. Because of this, when (not if) things get tough because the oil has run out, the British will be exceptionally vulnerable. The coming recession is going to be far worse than anything we've ever seen before. Without savings, life will be more difficult than it need have been.

Government policies have encouraged more and more people to spend every penny they can lay their hands on – and every penny they can borrow too. By 2007, Brown's policies had encouraged the British people to accumulate personal debt of £1,300 billion (much of it backed by loans taken against the increasing value of residential housing).

Gordon is a Moron

Thanks to Gordon Brown's years of high tax, wasteful spending and egregious incompetence, real incomes in Britain are stagnant while household debt has reached 164% of annual disposable income – the highest figure in the developed world.

Brown never showed any signs of caring a jot about investors. It seemed to me as though he thought there was something evil in saving for hard times or old age. (Though his policies have created problems galore and anyone living in a Brown designed economy who doesn't save is certifiably reckless).Brown created a highly regulated world but although his regulations made life difficult, complex and expensive for investors they didn't provide any protection.

What are the regulations for? Well, they're part of Brown's nanny mentality. Gordon always has to interfere and control. It's the fascist in him.

The Labour Party has proved itself unconcerned about the rights of the individual and of shareholders and investors in general. In October 2001, the Government pushed the company Railtrack into administration knowing that this would cause hardship to many small shareholders. This wicked act caused much resentment, particularly when it became known that the shareholders had been dismissed as 'grannies' and of little political significance.

The Government's regulators have proved woefully incapable of protecting investors, as millions of investors discovered when the huge pension company Equitable Life got into trouble. Considering the amount of red tape Brown has wrapped around the whole financial services industry (much of it laughably said to have been designed to prevent terrorism and money laundering) investors might have reasonably expected that the upside might be that their savings would be protected from incompetence, theft and stupidity. Not a bit of it.

When the European Parliament discussed the British Government's handling of the Equitable Life disaster, a remarkable 89% of MEPs voted in support of a report damning Brown and the rest of the British Government for their handling of the situation.

Other investors who had entrusted their savings to zero dividend preference shares also discovered that the Government had little interest in, or concern for, the rights of small shareholders.

It was disgraceful, unforgivable acts like these (together with Brown's raid on pension funds) which forced many people into putting their savings into buy-to-let property, rather than more traditional investments. And this, of course, helped push up the price of houses in Britain.

★ ★ ★

The UK is one of the largest stock markets in the world. Under Gordon Brown's Chancellorship it has been one of the very worst performers in the world. Shares have done worse in Britain since 1997 than just about anywhere else in the world. Between 1997 and 2004, share values in Britain shrank by 0.1% a year (compared to an annual rise of 4.2% in the USA and 5.1% in France for example). The stock market in Britain has now risen 56% since 1997 but it has significantly under-performed other markets. Over the same time the USA has gained 104%. EU regulations cannot be blamed for Britain's failure because the rest of Europe has risen 158%. Brown's raid on pension funds helped destroy pensions, companies and shares. It was a truly vicious circle. And Brown's spending spree has taken billions out of the wealth creating private sector. And, of course, red tape has slowed things down and made everything more expensive. It should worry Brown's supporters to know that historical evidence shows that a strong stock market predicts strong economic growth.

It is of no little significance that UK listed companies have lagged the rest of the world when it comes to profit. Since 1997, the earnings per share on the UK market has risen by 75% compared with 115% for the USA and 250% for the rest of Europe.

Today, many investment portfolios are, thanks to Gordon, still where they were in 1997. In a decade where the State has grown rapidly, many investors have had ten years of zero growth.

Chapter Twenty One

Global Warming:
An Opportunity For More Taxes

'When a long train of abuses and usurpations...evinces a design to reduce them (the people) under absolute despotism, it is their right, it is their duty, to throw off such government.'
THOMAS JEFFERSON, USA DECLARATION OF INDEPENDENCE

Brown, like other British politicians, has for years claimed to be concerned about environmental issues, and to regard global warming as a serious problem. It was the Treasury, under Gordon Brown, which commissioned the Stern report, the alarming and firm conclusions of which they say we should all take very seriously.

But the one real move the Government made to control global warming was to introduce new air travel taxes. These were pretty obviously designed not to cut air travel but to bring in more money. He should have put a tax on flights not on tickets – but that might not have brought in as much money.

His so-called green tax is just a cash cow.

The harsh reality is that while Gordon Brown was Chancellor, British air travel grew at the horrifying rate of 13% a year. Worst of all Brown did nothing to control internal UK flights. There are 37 flights a day from London to Manchester and hundreds more from London to places like Leeds and Newcastle. There are many flights to Paris too. All these flights are unnecessary because there are excellent rail links available. Improving (even subsidising) the railways would do far more to prevent global warming. Instead, the Government has deliberately created dependence on unsustainable, irresponsible, short haul flights by doing nothing to improve other forms of transport. British trains are now among the most expensive in the world and prices seem destined to rise ever higher.

Moreover, members of the Labour Party have not cut back their own flying, and the Government has consistently refused to tell others not to fly (probably because they are worried about the short-term political unpopularity that would accompany such an instruction).

The Labour Party has consistently told us that we should turn off our lights, not leave TV sets on stand-by and limit our use of cars and aeroplanes in order to cut down on our carbon emissions (in order to reduce global warming) but the waste produced by Government departments rises annually. The waste produced by DEFRA – the British Government Department responsible for the environment, food and rural affairs – went up by 20% in 2005 when compared to the previous year. Most British Government Departments are using energy less efficiently than they did before New Labour came to power. Emissions from Department of Transport vehicles have risen by 40% since 2002. The Home Office officially produced 17,697 tons of rubbish in 2005 – that's 63% more than in 2004. (Some people might say, with justification, that everything the Home Office produces is rubbish.) Businesses and individuals are reducing their waste. But not the Government. More than half of British Government Departments and agencies are failing to meet the British Government's own recycling targets. They are increasing not reducing their output of carbon emissions. And during 2006, the use of cars by Government ministers climbed by 20% on the previous year.

With Brown as Chancellor it was clear that the Government simply wasn't serious about protecting the environment. Every new piece of environmental legislation introduced made things worse not better. And every piece of new legislation that was supposed to protect the environment was, in reality, simply yet another stealth tax. Frightening people about global warming was just another excuse for raising more money.

Most people agree with this thought. In March 2007, 60% of the British population thought that the British Government was using climate change as an excuse to put up taxes.

Most stupidly of all, the British Government is closing 2,500 Post Offices. These closures will inevitably result in a massive waste of energy, an increase in congestion, an increase in the queues at the remaining Post Offices (and, therefore, reduced productivity), an increase in pollution, and an increase in global warming. The number of village Post Offices has crashed since Brown took over the Treasury in 1997. When the village Post Office goes, the village shop invariably goes with it (because they are usually the same establishment). Hundreds of thousands of people now have to drive miles to buy a stamp or a loaf of bread. The Government has banned Post Offices from handling pensions and allowances and, as a direct result, the system is losing money.

Once the Labour Party got into power in 1997, they started closing rural post offices with unprecedented zeal. Between 1997 and 2007 they closed 4,000. In 2007, the Government ordered the closure of another 2,500 Post Offices – mostly in rural areas. In just one decade the Labour Government will have closed a third of a network of local Post Offices which took over a century to put together, and which has been a major backbone of social life in Britain.

If Brown really cared about preventing global warming he would have ensured that local Post Offices stayed open. This would not have been difficult. All he had to do was to ensure that anyone claiming benefits of any kind had to obtain them through a Post Office rather than through a bank. The big commercial banks make huge amounts of money out of handling benefit and pension payments on behalf of the Government. That money could have gone to the Post Offices.

★ ★ ★

To suggest that putting our plastic bottles into one box and our tin cans in another is going to make any difference to the rate at which the earth heats up is bizarre. The truth, of course, is that the

Government is introducing new rules about the way we dispose of our rubbish as an excuse to push up taxes, to frighten us, to bully us and to introduce yet more legislation. In many areas local councils now collect rubbish once a fortnight. They fine those who leave out too much rubbish, put their rubbish out on the wrong day or fail to close the lids of their bins.

Local rubbish dumps are being equipped with spy cameras so that councils can see what people are throwing away. Authorities are doing this because they believe that when dustmen only collect once a fortnight (and households are limited to one or two bags per house) some people may be tempted to take extra rubbish to the local tip. Gosh. Councils in Britain are already fining people who overfill wheelie bins, put the wrong sort of rubbish in a rubbish container, put rubbish out on the wrong day, put personal rubbish in public collecting receptacles or fail to follow complex (and pointless) recycling rules. Microchips in rubbish bins enable councils to identify how much rubbish people throw away (and will, in due course, enable councils to charge householders for every pound of rubbish they discard). The new cameras at municipal tips will enable councils to check on who is throwing what away. In due course, bills will be sent out to householders who use public tips. 10,000 concealed cameras hidden in bin bags are being used to catch people putting their rubbish out on the wrong day. Offenders may face a fine of up to £1,000 so the cameras will presumably produce a good return. Dustmen will be warned which bag contains the camera so that they do not throw it in the rubbish by mistake. This, it was reported, is the latest method of using high-tech surveillance to reduce landfill.

None of this has anything to do with the environment. It was, let us not forget, Brown's new tax on landfill that forced many local authorities to scrap weekly rubbish collections.

The official policy on rubbish disposal, inspired by Brown's taxes, is causing massive increase in rats and mice. There has been a 39% increase in call-outs to rat catchers in areas of Britain where fortnight collections have been introduced.

Several local authority spokesidiots have said that citizens should double wrap all their rubbish in plastic bags in order to avoid attracting rats. It presumably does not occur to them that all this extra wrapping increases the energy consumed and wasted. Another spokesidiot said that people should only eat fish (which goes off very quickly) on the day before their rubbish was due to be collected. Some local councils now refuse to allow people to take rubbish to the official council dump unless they take it to the dump in a motorcar. People who turn up carrying their rubbish for recycling are turned away. The councils which do this presumably believe that driving to a rubbish dump is more energy efficient than walking there.

The Government blames the new rubbish collecting rules on EU regulations. I love blaming the EU for the crazy things it does but rubbish in France is collected daily (including Sundays and bank holidays) and, as far as I know, France is still a member of the EU.

The Environmental Agency published a 209-page report in 2006 showing that disposable nappies are no worse for the planet than cloth ones which have to be laundered in hot water and detergent and then dried. The emissions are the same.

The Government wants council workmen (such as dustmen) to have access to police intelligence so that they can help the authorities more effectively. The police will, of course, have access to the NHS database which will, when the snags have been removed, hold confidential medical information about every man, woman and child in the country. So dustmen and other council workers will shortly have access to your medical records.

Some local authorities have already announced that they have authorised their staff to rummage through rubbish to make sure that the right bits of rubbish have been put in the correct containers. Councils claim that they are entitled to go through the rubbish that people throw out, and that they need to do this in order to identify miscreants who haven't sorted their bank statements from their yoghurt pots with due care and attention. Linked to this is the fact that some councils refuse to take away material which has been shredded. (Presumably because it is more difficult to discover identifying material when documents have been shredded. Shredding is, of course, a vital way to protect the integrity of sensitive information.) If the wrong rubbish is found in the wrong container the binmen are encouraged to take out identifying documents (such as bank statements and private letters) so that people can be identified and legal action can be taken. Why is allowing council employees to peek at bank statements not a direct breach of a good deal of Data Protection legislation and probably the Human Rights Act too? And what about the risk of dustmen using their new rights to steal and sell identity information Shred everything you put in your rubbish that can identify you – including envelopes.– thereby facilitating identity theft and terrorism? In the rush to comply with Brown's new rules on landfill, such problems are dismissed without hesitation. It is surely an infringement of my human rights for binmen and other council employees to forage amidst my rubbish looking to see whether I've put the right stuff in the right bins.

> British households recycled around 150,000 tonnes of food and drink cans last year. That's about 2% of the total ferrous scrap recycled in the UK. Far more ferrous material was dropped in that same period on Iraq and Afghanistan. If the Government really wanted to cut down waste they wouldn't start so many wars.

It is a myth that there is a shortage of landfill sites and that we need to tax their use more highly. Putting aside the fact that Britain imports rubbish from America (and the Government is keen to allow the Americans to dump their most dangerous waste in Britain) the truth is that there are still plenty of quarries and mines in Britain that need to be filled. The amount of stuff going into landfill sites from domestic users is a tiny proportion of the amount going in from industrial users. There is plenty of room and no need to limit it or tax it. Even the Government has admitted that there is no shortage of space in the UK for the dumping of rubbish.

It is sometimes better to incinerate waste than to recycle it. Crisp packets, yoghurt pots and meal trays aren't worth recycling. Collecting and cleaning them takes up far more energy than it saves. It's far more energy efficient to incinerate them in power generating plants that make energy from waste.

Much of the paper and plastic so lovingly collected in Britain is then shipped out to China to be recycled. Unless it is sent there on wind-powered yachts it is difficult to see how this can possibly be considered energy efficient. Incinerating paper, on the other hand, is carbon neutral because living matter sucks up carbon dioxide from the air while it is growing – just as much as it emits while being burned. It makes more sense to incinerate used paper in an energy-from-waste plant and to import fresh paper from Northern Europe where paper plants use non-fossil fuels for power generation. The net effect of burning is a reduction in carbon dioxide emissions.

★ ★ ★

Our recycling efforts make no discernible difference to our annual emissions. If people wanted to make a real difference they would have to make big sacrifices. They would need to reduce their consumption of goods and electricity. They would need to wear the same clothes until they fell apart, and to use their television sets until they broke down and could not be repaired. No parents should ever take children to school in a car. (They should walk with them or go on bicycles.) No one should fly anywhere. People should all eat mass-produced meals in cheap cafes and wash once a week to save hot water.

If the Government really wanted to discourage waste and to stop global warming they would subsidise the repair and renovation of things like TV sets and vacuum cleaners. This would be infinitely more useful than all the recycling we're being forced to do. But the EU, the Government and local councils all make loads of money out of the recycling con. And it gives them a lot of chances to smother us with even more laws and taxes.

Recycling has nothing to do with the environment or global warming. It's all about laws and taxes. The authorities know that recycling much of the rubbish that is carefully sorted costs more than it saves. And so all those carefully sorted boxes are often simply tipped together into one landfill.

★ ★ ★

During the English floods of July 2007, Gordon Brown was doing his very best to show sympathy but avoid responsibility. His spin-doctors produced a flood-risk guru who claimed that the flooding, the destruction of homes and businesses and all the rest of it was the result of inadequate sewers. This enabled local councils, the Environment Agency, the Government and Brown to disclaim all responsibility and to blame the Victorian engineers who built (what were, at the time, perfectly adequate) sewers and the water companies who now manage them.

Brown's spin-doctors presumably breathed a huge sigh of relief and scurried back to their luxurious (and dry) offices in Downing Street and Whitehall glowing with the pride of a job well done. They had side-stepped around the problem of several billion pounds worth of damage and avoided criticism for cutting the flood defence budget and allowing building on flood plains by promising £14 million of aid. As we all know the £14 million will probably never be paid anyway and, even if it is, will probably just come out of an existing budget for something else.

Typically sneaky stuff. Tony Blair would have been proud.

But if the flooding occurred because the sewers were inadequate (as the Government's tame experts say it did) then the flooding was Gordon Brown's fault.

Here are some very simple facts which prove that Brown, and no one else, has to take responsibility for all those damp carpets, all those ruined kitchens, all those floating cars and all the mayhem and misery caused by the floods.

1. The water companies are only allowed to spend their customers' money on repairs and renewals if an organisation called Ofwat says they can. (There are, of course, organisations controlling everything these days. They are all described as independent but most of them are as independent as Scotland. Ofwat controls water.)

2. When he was Chancellor of the Exchequer, Gordon Brown told Ofwat to keep the water bills down but to tell the water companies to repair their leaky pipes and to stop wasting water. So Ofwat wisely did as the Chancellor ordered.

3. The water companies duly spent some money on replacing

clean water pipes (to cut down the embarrassing leakage and waste) and kept their prices down as they had been ordered. Naturally, this meant that there wasn't any money left for repairing or upgrading sewers.

4. When the entirely predictable heavy rains hit England in 2007, Brown started thrashing around looking for someone to blame. (Brown knew that the storms were predicted. As Chancellor he had, after all, introduced special taxes on airline flights which were inspired by the spectre of global warming. He could have spent the taxes he had raised on protecting people from flooding. He didn't.) Naturally, Brown insisted that the flooding wasn't his fault or his responsibility or anything to do with him at all. He was miles away at the time. And, besides, the floods occurred in England and he's Scottish. But, when you peel away the layers of spin and look at the facts it is clear that the flooding was Gordon Brown's fault.

Chapter Twenty Two
Squeezing The Poor Until The Pips Squeak

'There is no art which one government sooner learns from another than that of draining money from the pockets of the people.'
ADAM SMITH

Brown's policies have created a world of four quarters:

1. The people who work for the Government in some form of administrative role (these are the only ones with security of tenure and guaranteed pensions).

2. The people who rely on 'benefits' of one kind or another.

3. The people who are working in the city and, by taking advantage of Gordon's astonishingly generous tax regime for hedge fund managers and private equity profiteers, are making an absolute fortune without ever doing anything truly useful. Brown has created a society in which it is possible for a relatively small number of people (mainly either foreigners or people working in the hedge fund and private equity industry) to become enormously rich. The year 2006, the last of Brown's tenure as Chancellor, was a record-breaking year for the super rich. By January 2007, there were 68 billionaires based in the UK, and the 1,000 richest people in the country had increased their collective wealth by 20% in just a single year. Inequality has widened dramatically under Brown. The

2007 bonus season saw 3,000 City of London bankers receive bonuses of £1 million or more. (That is, a bonus on top of their already massive salaries.) Gordon Brown doesn't seem as disturbed by this as are many taxpayers. Indeed, after ten years of Brown's tinkering and complicating the system it seems that he prefers to squeeze the middle classes rather than inconvenience the mega-rich, and Labour has surprised many by being (in the words of Peter Mandelson) 'intensely relaxed about people getting filthy rich'. And the Labour Party has surprised people even more by showing itself uninterested in getting the filthy rich to pay their taxes.

4. The hard working, highly taxed, insecure remainder who are the ones whose work and taxes pay for everything else.

Brown, of course, has claimed to be committed to reducing poverty. His actions have proved that to be a terminological inexactitude, for the gap between the poor and the rich is now at its widest for 40 years, according to a report by the Joseph Rowntree Foundation.

Despite his promises, and his alleged affection for the principles of socialism, Brown has created an absurd world in which the rich have got richer and the poor have got poorer. The people getting rich are no longer hard working entrepreneurs or efficient company managers but financial engineers, private equity experts and hedge fund managers. A lucky minority has been getting exceedingly, absurdly rich, thanks to Brown. They have been getting rich by charging huge, unprecedented fees for managing other people's money, by using tax laws to their advantage and by encouraging the middle classes to take on increasing amounts of debt.

Thanks to Gordon Brown's years of wasteful spending and egregious incompetence, real incomes among British people who work for a living (as opposed to sitting in Parliament or receiving benefits) are stagnant, while household debt has reached 164% of annual disposable income – the highest figure in the developed world. Brown has introduced steep tax increases for the poor and the middle classes. Brown's 2007 budget meant that people earning over £40,000 a year benefited most while those earning less than £18,000 were worse off.

Brown claimed to be committed to eradicating poverty but only the rich benefited under his Chancellorship. It has been reported that there are super rich people in Britain who pay less tax than their cleaners. (Private equity millionaires negotiated a special exemption from the Labour Government – effectively allowing them to pay tax at 10%.) On the other hand there are now 175,000 children in Britain looking after their parents or another relative. The billions pumped into the NHS have done nothing for them (though they have enriched thousands of new Stalinist bureaucrats.) Perhaps Brown is only committed to eradicating poverty in the Brown household.

★ ★ ★

Politicians constantly tell us that we are all getting richer. Ever since Harold Macmillan, politicians have been assuring us that 'we've never had it so good'.

But the evidence suggests that, as usual, the politicians are lying. Some people are getting much, much richer than they were, but most of us are not better off than we were five, ten, fifteen or even thirty years ago. In fact, however you measure things, most of us are worse off. If you adjust incomes for real levels of inflation, the average wage is less now than it was decades ago. According to the International Monetary Fund the percentage of Gross Domestic Product (GDP) going to workers in the G7 countries has fallen over the last 20 years. Instead of being shared out among the workers, the profits have been distributed among a very small number of super-rich people.

It is perhaps not surprising that the *Financial Times* now produces a supplement called *How To Spend It*. Nor is it much of a surprise that an index of 'bling' and luxury companies has shown a massive rise in the last few years.

We may seem to have more money but the cost of houses, fuel and heating has rocketed, and the fact that our currency is constantly being devalued means that most of us are working harder (and having to put up with an unfriendlier, unhealthier lifestyle) but taking home less money than our parents did. Savings have collapsed because, after taxes, people don't have enough money left over to put anything aside for a 'rainy day' – and can't see the point in saving anyway. Most people now live right on the edge and are in no position to deal with any sort of crisis.

The people getting rich are the ones working in the financial services industry – private equity and hedge funds. Ten years ago, graduates all wanted to be dot com millionaires. A survey of American college graduates in 1999 showed that many had decided that they would retire within five years as multi-millionaires. Becoming obscenely rich had become a career plan.

Now, thanks to Gordon Brown, young British graduates are all keen to work for hedge funds or private equity houses. That's where the billions are waiting to be collected these days.

Young graduates don't want to create wealth – they just want to redistribute it, taking it from widows and orphans and stuffing it into their own pockets.

The modern, successful man (or woman) in Brown's Britain doesn't produce anything you can see. He doesn't make anything you can eat, or read or sit on. He doesn't sell tea or make toothpaste. He doesn't edit a newspaper or make films. All these activities involve red tape, endless legislation and high taxes.

Thanks to Gordon Brown, today's successful citizens are money magicians. They move money from A to B and takes a huge cut for their labours. They borrow money from C and lend it to D. They borrow from E to buy F which they then sell to G for a huge profit. This isn't just usury. It's gone far past moneylending. It's a huge game of pass the parcel. Along the way everyone who plays is a winner and everyone takes a cut. And, thanks to the special deal they've cut with Gordon, all the winners pay tax at just 10%.

In the current financial year, there are expected to be 30,000 individuals in Britain earning more than £500,000. Nearly all of them work in London. Most of them work in the 'financial services' industry. A good chunk are lawyers. Doubtless, a few are retired politicians. The salaries of business bosses have been dragged up by these absurd salaries. The average Chief Executive Officer in the UK now earns 100 times as much as the average worker.

Brown's policies have made London the most expensive city on the planet. It's officially the most expensive city in which to buy property, the most expensive city in which to live and the most expensive city to visit.

In 2007, Prince William, heir to the English throne and an example to the young, was reported to have spent £5,000 on booze in a single night in a nightclub.

The three most popular countries for rich sportsmen to choose as home are Monaco, Switzerland and Britain. Of the three, the most tax advantageous (for non-British sportsmen) is Britain.

Thanks to a bizarre tax system which punishes those Britons who work for their money and encourages non-domiciled foreign residents to regard the UK as a tax haven, Britain has become two nations.

The unfairness and stupidity of the rules which enable foreigners to avoid UK taxes is easy to illustrate.

If a Briton left the UK and went to live in, say, France for five years he could acquire citizenship of that country, giving up his British citizenship in the process. He could, then, presumably, move back to the UK for the rest of his life without having to pay tax. I wonder how many Britons would regard five years of pleasant exile as a sensible price to pay for a lifetime without paying taxes? Would this work? I can't see why not, though I dare say the authorities might think of a way to stop it.

★ ★ ★

Despite combined sales of more than £12 billion, and operating profits of more than £400 million, five of the ten largest private equity owned companies in the UK paid not one penny in UK corporation tax in 2005/6. Indeed, on the contrary, the companies received £11 million corporation tax credit from the Government.

Seven out of the ten richest people in Britain are foreigners who either pay no tax at all or else pay very little tax (in many cases paying tax, with Gordon's approval and connivance, at a 10% rate). Britain is (with the USA) one of the world's most popular tax havens for non-domiciled residents and one of the two most popular places for money laundering.

There are nearly two million foreigners living in the UK who pay no UK taxes at all unless they want to. Non-domiciled residents pay no tax on their income from abroad unless they bring that income into the UK. This isn't something new; its been this way in the UK since income tax was introduced. Originally, the rule applied to all taxpayers. But, since 1914, the rule has only applied to foreigners living in the UK. Now the 1.7 million foreigners living tax free in the UK don't even have to file tax returns.

At the Labour Party conference in 1994, three years before he became Chancellor of the Exchequer, Gordon Brown announced that a Labour Government would tighten up residency rules for the rich. His words were that Labour would 'rewrite the tax rules for the undeserving rich'. I have no doubt he got big cheers from Labour Party stalwarts.

But Brown has done nothing to change the rules.

Coincidentally, Labour receives huge financial support from wealthy foreigners who live in the UK but pay no tax.

For many wealthy foreigners, Britain is now a tax haven – they don't pay tax on any income which is not earned in, or brought into, the UK. In practice this means that they live in Britain but don't pay tax. They are exempt from Capital Gains Tax and Inheritance Tax.

Moreover, they can use offshore trusts to cut the stamp duty they pay when they buy a house. If a British taxpayer buys a £5 million house in London he will pay stamp duty of £200,000. If a non-domiciled foreigner buys the same house via an offshore trust he will pay just £25,000 in tax. So British taxpayers pay more for British houses than foreigners do. This system is unique to Britain. It's hardly surprising that more than half of London's multi-million pound houses are now bought by wealthy foreigners who don't pay British tax and it's hardly surprising that London house prices keep soaring. (The cost of all housing is then dragged upwards – with the result that young couples can't afford to buy a house at all.)

While encouraging free-loading foreigners to regard Britain as a tax haven, Brown has stamped down hard on any British taxpayer who might put a foot on foreign territory.

Under Gordon's patronage, the Inland Revenue decided to have a crackdown on Britons holding offshore accounts. They forced banks to give them the names and addresses of customers holding accounts in other countries (concepts such as privacy and confidentiality are alien to New Labour) and then threatened to hound the customers they identified in order to raise some extra cash. The theory was, presumably, that thousands of Britons were stashing money in offshore accounts and not declaring it. The reality was that most of the accounts were probably held by Britons needing a way to pay the gas and electricity bills for their French or Spanish bolt holes.

Inevitably, the scheme seems to have backfired.

In 2004/5, just 112,000 people living in Britain declared themselves to be living in Britain but non-domiciled for tax purposes.

According to *Moneyweek* magazine more than 200,000 people are expected to claim non-domicile tax status for 2006/7.

So, thanks to Brown's over-belligerent attitude, the Treasury now has to face the fact that the number of people living in Britain who are able to avoid income and Capital Gains Tax has probably doubled.

Another magnificent blunder by Gordon the Moron.

Curiously, Gordon the Moron is so proud of Britain's status as a tax haven that the Government actually boasts about it. Britain is being promoted as a tax haven on the Government's 'UK Trade and Investment' web site, highlighting the unusually generous tax benefits for foreign residents. 'It (Britain) is also perhaps the only tax haven which has the high degree of respectability sought by the international business community', says the British Government reassuringly.

And it was, remember, Gordon Brown who promised that the Labour Party would tighten up on residency rules for rich foreigners.

Epilogue

Now that Gordon is no longer Chancellor, Government spending is going to have to fall and taxes are going to have to rise.

Spending will have to fall for several reasons.

First, the PFI initiative so loved by Gordon has lumbered the nation with massive debts and huge ongoing costs.

Second, Gordon's massive tax increases, bizarre regulations and aggressive attitude towards honest taxpayers has forced hundreds of thousands of honest citizens out of the country. Every year around 500,000 immigrants pour into Britain. Some of them will work. Many of them will rely on the State to survive. At the same time as those 500,000 people come into Britain, 300,000 leave – heading off for Australia, France, South Africa, Italy and Germany. The ones leaving are hard working, middle class taxpayers. And so the nation's tax take is falling dramatically each year.

Third, Brown has presided over a massive increase in Government hiring. And he has, therefore, dramatically increased the Government's salary and pension responsibilities.

Fourth, Blair's Wars have cost the nation billions of much needed money. And the extra security costs which have resulted from the fact that Blair's Wars have made Britain the world's primary terrorist target will also weaken the economy.

The cuts in spending are going to be very noticeable. There is going to be far less money available for health, education and every other Government department. And, with vast numbers of salaries to be met, what money is available will have to be used to pay wages and pensions. There will be very little, if any, extra money for patients, pupils or repairs. There will, I predict, be a significant drop in real average annual spending growth. There will, within a year or two, even be a drop in annual spending. And the number of new PFI projects will fall. Many of those which have already been announced will be quietly cancelled. (New roads, and road improvements, will probably be the first to go. Politicians don't regard roads as big vote-winners and so, by and large, they don't bother spending much money on them.)

Having moved on from the Treasury, Gordon Brown will doubtless be able to blame someone else for mismanaging the nation's finances.

And then there's the oil.

We are using the stuff up faster than we are finding new supplies. The one thing that the experts agree on is that when we run out of oil we will all be in big trouble. And, thanks to Gordon Brown's economic policies, Britain is, of all the developed countries in the world, the least well-prepared and the most vulnerable. By overspending on public services, by building up a huge national debt, by overtaxing, by expanding the civil service by nearly a million people, by dramatically increasing the number of people entirely dependent on the State, by introducing so much red tape and such complicated tax legislation that entrepreneurs are discouraged from starting new businesses, by destroying pensions and discouraging savings, by forcing 'targets' on hospitals, schools and everyone else, and by creating an unprecedented housing boom, Gordon the Moron has weakened Britain enormously. By pushing up inflation (and fiddling the figures so as to pretend that he hadn't) and, encouraging citizens to live on debt, Gordon has, I suspect, done more long-lasting damage to Britain than even Hitler managed.

Brown has created a political and economic environment which can only survive if there is massive growth. Without growth there will be no increase in the Government's tax revenue. And without a steady and considerable increase in tax revenue the Government will be unable to meet its financial commitments or pay its considerable debts. Our national debt is now so great (thanks to Brown's incompetent management of the economy) that Britain cannot survive comfortably without economic growth.

And for real economic growth we need to continue to use, and rely on, vast amounts of oil. What is left of our industry relies on oil. We cannot export without oil. We cannot make things without oil. Our society is so dependent upon the oil we import that without oil our society will crumble.

Does Brown not realise that the oil is running out? Just how moronic can a moron get?

Brown has put Britain into a position where we must either choose to go into a recession, and then into a deep depression, or wait and allow ourselves to be pushed into recession and depression when the oil starts to run out.

A recession we choose will, of course, be much easier to manage than a recession that is forced upon us.

The former would be painful.

The latter would lead to mass unemployment, widespread rioting and political revolution.

That's the future Gordon Brown has guaranteed.

And I believe that there is a very real chance that the British Government could go bust when the oil crisis really starts to bite. Governments, like businesses, need to balance their income and their outgoings. Thanks to Gordon Brown's tenure as Chancellor, Britain is hugely in debt. And, because of Brown's long-term borrowings and long-term pension commitments, this debt is likely to continue to increase.

There is a limit to how much taxes can be raised. In the end, the high earners will all leave the country. The only people left will be the ones claiming benefits and pensions – and on the Government payroll.

At that point the country will go bust. The currency will collapse. And all bets are off.

Those seemingly golden pensions guaranteed to civil servants will suddenly look rather unattractive. The Government simply won't be able to meet its commitments. And if it tries to do so by printing more money (which it probably will) then inflation will go through the roof.

As inflation rises so interest rates will be forced up. As interest rates go up so house prices will go down. And as house prices fall the banks will start calling in some of their loans. More and more people will go bust. Consumer spending will fall. Shops will suffer. The number of people with real jobs will collapse. The amount of money available for spending at the hairdressers will collapse.

But Gordon Brown's vast army of Government employees will still have their jobs. And they will still need to be paid. And the millions who have retired, or chosen to go off on long-term sick leave suffering from stress, will still want to be paid.

And so taxes will have to go up.

And people will have even less money to spend on having their hair done.

Anyone who tells you that Britain is booming and that the future is rosy is either certifiably insane or a liar.

It is when inflation gets really out of control that things will become very nasty.

Many young people don't remember the days when inflation hit double figures and interest rates charged by reputable companies were 15%, 16%, 17% or even more. In the 1980s, after a decade of high inflation and ever rising interest rates, investors happily snatched offers of long-term financing at fixed rates of 11% and 12%. Such rates seemed like a bargain.

It has happened many times in history.

And it will happen again.

When inflation soars and interest rates rocket but wages stay constant, the whole economy suffers. People worry about every small expenditure. The grocery bill soars each week. And luxuries become a thing of the past. Big new purchases (houses, cars, television sets and so on) are postponed indefinitely.

At times of high inflation the people who run businesses become wary. And when interest rates are high it doesn't pay to borrow money to expand. No one hires new staff. Existing jobs disappear.

High inflation rates mean that savings are eroded. If inflation rates dramatically exceed interest rates (as can, and will happen) cash in the bank or building society loses its purchasing power. Investments in shares will be a disaster too. As companies struggle to survive so dividends will dry up and share prices will collapse. Anyone who tries to survive by buying an index fund, and trusting that the market as a whole will survive, will lose money. Investors who have grown accustomed to the idea of buying a diversified portfolio and sitting back with a self-satisfied grin will suffer great pain as they see their savings melt away.

As the oil price goes up the problems of our world will, for a while, resemble the temporary problems of the 1970s. High inflation, high interest rates, high unemployment and falling house prices will, I believe, combine to create great misery among those who are not properly prepared.

Investment policies which worked well in the 1990s or the early part of the twenty first century will fail miserably. Savings, nest eggs and pension plans will evaporate.

In the past, Government employees have always been pretty well immune to the horrors of a collapsing economy. Their jobs and salaries were safe, as were their pensions.

But this will change.

As the oil price rises, rises and rises again, and the economy falters and starts to collapse, the Government's income will no longer be sufficient to pay the bills.

When the oil really does start to run out there will be a massive rise in the number of bankruptcies – particularly among small firms. Since half the people in Britain are employed by small firms, the incidence of unemployment will rocket still higher.

China will quickly suffer because America and Europe will have less money to spend on television sets.

Paradoxically, this may, for a while, have a deflationary effect on prices. Television sets made in China will cost less and less as Chinese manufacturers struggle to stay in business and to keep their inventories at manageable levels.

But, despite frequent rises in taxes, the Government's income will fall. Fewer people will be earning and so fewer people will be paying tax. The Government will have to reduce its spending.

The problem, of course, is that much Government spending is fixed because of the commitment to pay pensions to retired civil servants. During his ten years as Chancellor of the Exchequer, Brown helped create nearly a million new public sector jobs – all with fat, final salary pensions. These were not vital employees serving the public. We're talking about well-paid jobs for a Deputy Outreach Worker's Assistant Coordinator For Nappy Training. The result will be that all services will deteriorate and taxes will rise remorselessly – until they can rise no more.

At this point Government spending will rocket again because of the cost of paying benefits to millions more who have joined the list of the unemployed.

Whoever is Chancellor will have a constant problem balancing the books. Gordon Brown's terrible legacy – debt, debt and more debt – will become clear at last. Public spending will have to fall dramatically and all services provided by the Government (roads, schools, hospitals and so on) will deteriorate day by day, week by week and month by month. The Government will probably introduce special fees for providing basic services.

And the Government will, of course, raise taxes again.

Even though services are in constant decline income taxes, corporate taxes, Capital Gains Taxes, National Insurance, VAT and stealth taxes will all go up.

But, eventually, there will come a point when taxes cannot rise any more.

And then the unthinkable will happen.

The Government will have to start laying off vast numbers of civil servants. And then it will find itself unable to pay pensions to those civil servants who are already retired.

For a while the Government will try to borrow enough money to fulfil its obligations. But this won't work. Where can a bankrupt Government borrow money?

What will be happening in Britain will be happening elsewhere. Other Governments will be struggling to survive. If the Government tries to print its way out of trouble the currency will collapse. And Britain will resemble Germany in the 1920s.

Does Gordon Brown know how stupid he is and how much trouble he has created for Britain?

I suspect not.

Indeed, I rather suspect that he thinks he's bright. I believe he thinks he's brighter than he is.

Gordon destroyed Britain because he is a moron.

And it's because he is a moron that he still doesn't realise how much damage he has done.

Brown has failed miserably to prepare the nation for the coming oil shortage – a crisis that will permanently change our world.

Biography Of The Author

Vernon Coleman was an angry young man for as long as it was decently possible. He then turned into an angry middle-aged man. And now, with no effort whatsoever, he has matured into being an angry old man. He is, he confesses, just as angry as he ever was. Indeed, he may be even angrier because, he says, the more he learns about life the more things he finds to be angry about.

Cruelty, prejudice and injustice are the three things most likely to arouse his well-developed sense of ire but he admits that, at a pinch, inefficiency, incompetence and greed will do almost as well.

The author has an innate dislike of taking orders and a pathological contempt for pomposity, hypocrisy and the sort of unthinking political correctness which attracts support from *Guardian* reading pseudo-intellectuals. He also has a passionate loathing for those in authority who do not understand that unless their authority is tempered with compassion and a sense of responsibility the end result must always be an extremely unpleasant brand of totalitarianism.

He upsets more people than he means to but apologises only to those who are upset by accident rather than design.

He likes books, cafés and writing and has never been much of an athlete, though he once won a certificate for swimming a width of the public baths in Walsall (which was, at the time, in Staffordshire but has now, apparently, been moved elsewhere).

He doesn't like yappy dogs, big snarly dogs with saliva dripping from their fangs or people who think that wearing a uniform automatically gives them status and rights. He likes trains, dislikes planes and used to like cars until some idiot invented speed cameras, bus lanes and car parks where the spaces are so narrow that only the slimmest, and tinniest of vehicles will fit in.

He likes cats, pens and notebooks and used to like watching cricket until the authorities sold out and allowed people to paint slogans on the grass. His favourite place is Les Invalides, his favourite author is P.G.Wodehouse and his favourite piece of music is whatever he is listening to at the time (because that's why he put it on).

He enjoys chess, malt whisky and old films and is devoted to Donna Antoinette who is the kindest, sweetest, most sensitive woman a man could hope to meet and who, as an undeserved but welcome bonus, makes the very best roast potatoes on the planet.

For a catalogue of Vernon Coleman's books
please write to:

Publishing House
Trinity Place
Barnstaple
Devon EX32 9HG
England

Telephone   01271 328892
Fax   01271 328768

Outside the UK:
Telephone   +44 1271 328892
Fax   +44 1271 328768

Or visit our web site:

www.vernoncoleman.com

Also by Vernon Coleman

The O.F.P.I.S. File

"The Most Powerful And Revealing Book About The EU Ever Published"

- Were we taken into the EU illegally?
- The EU and our money
- Fraud in the EU
- The EU's regionalisation of Britain
- The EU, the law and your disappearing freedom
- The EU is destroying business
- The damage done by the British Government 'gold-plating' EU legislation
- It's the EU that insists we carry ID cards
- The EU's policy on immigration: a ticking time bomb
- The EU and the stupidity of the biofuels directive
- The failure of the media to inform us about the EU
- The Lisbon Treaty, the EU Constitution, the Queen, a good many lies and the end of Britain
- Why the EU is just like the old USSR
- Why English (and British) history is being suppressed
- The case for leaving the EU: why England should declare independence

"Had to thank you and praise you for your incredible work getting out your informative book on the EU." (M.W., WALES)

"I have just finished reading my latest Vernon Coleman book, *The OFPIS File*, and think it probably the best yet, not only because it lights up the EU scam in a way that few can, but has such a great deal of relevant detail." (J.M., LANCS)

"Thank you for sending me your *OFPIS* book which I managed to read in about two days flat. Your books are very readable and are hard to put down once started (the secret must lie in your writing style)." (A.K., MIDDLESEX)

"Vernon Coleman is well regarded in our circles as the author of several fine books exposing the machinations of the Europhile elite, and for others in which he emerges as a sincere and thoughtful English patriot. He most definitely is neither a crank nor an alarmist." IDENTITY MAGAZINE

"Whenever I read one of his books he never ceases to amaze me." (C.N., DORSET)

Published in paperback by Blue Books, price £15.99
Order from Publishing House • Trinity Place • Barnstaple • Devon
EX32 9HG • England
Telephone 01271 328892 • Fax 01271 328768

Also by Vernon Coleman

Oil Apocalypse

How to Survive, Protect Your Family And Profit Through The Coming Years of Crisis

Why the oil apocalypse is inevitable. How and why our dependence on oil will end in tears. And how you can prepare yourself and your family.
Also includes
* Our Unhealthy Addiction To A Gift Of Nature
* Peak Oil: The Beginning Of The End Of Civilisation
* Oil Wars: Past, Present And Future
* What Will Happen When The Oil Runs Out
* A New Energy Blueprint
* Your Personal Survival Plan
* Investing To Survive The Oil Apocalypse

The world you know is going to change dramatically and permanently. Anyone under fifty, with a normal life expectation, will live to see a world almost unrecognisable from the one they grew up in. Five billion people will die within a very short time. There will be no cars, no lorries, no buses, no aeroplanes and no supermarkets. The rich will travel by horse and cart. The middle classes will use bicycles. The poor will walk. The oil is running out and, as a result, our civilisation is reaching its end.

You will never read a more important or more alarming book than this one. The disaster inexorably heading our way will make any natural disaster, any tsunami, seem inconsequential. Forget global warming. Forget terrorism. They are trivial problems.

If you want to know the truth, and you think you can deal with it, sit down, turn to the first page and read this book now. It will change your life. Forever.

Vernon Coleman

Paperback £12.99
Published by Blue Books
Order from Publishing House • Trinity Place • Barnstaple •
Devon EX32 9HG • England
Telephone 01271 328892 • Fax 01271 328768
www.vernoncoleman.com

Also by Vernon Coleman

Living In A Fascist Country
Conspiracies, peak oil, greedy politicians, endless religious wars and your disappearing freedom and privacy.

We are losing our freedom and our privacy. The world is changing so fast that it is difficult to keep up. Britain and America are now fascist states. Why? What is going on? Whatever happened to democracy? Who is behind it all? How did we come to find ourselves in what the politicians boast will be an everlasting war?

'Everybody ought to have a copy of this book.'
FOURTH WORLD REVIEW

"I suggest you buy this book, to give you perspective on what's underway and what to do about it personally."
HARRY SCHULTZ "HSL NEWSLETTER"

'... like a bedtime book of nightmares ... scary stuff indeed.'
NEXUS

'With its accounts of how the government is fooling the people ... how ID cards and under-the-skin chips will destroy personal liberty, how public infrastructure has been offloaded to the highest bidder, and how the banks and other institutions are in on the take, this book is a manifesto aimed at alerting people to the fact that they're being manipulated big-time and calling on them to rise up to assert their rights before it's too late.'
NEXUS MAGAZINE

Paperback £15.99
Published by Blue Books
Order from Publishing House • Trinity Place • Barnstaple •
Devon EX32 9HG • England
Telephone 01271 328892 • Fax 01271 328768
www.vernoncoleman.com

Also by Vernon Coleman

How To Protect And Preserve Your Freedom, Identity And Privacy

Did you know that the average person does not know that their identity has been stolen until 12 months later? Did you know that the average person believes that shredding vital documents alone will protect them from fraud? And did you know that the average person believes that identity fraud will not happen to them?

Thousands of people fall victim to identity theft every year. The consequences can be absolutely devastating and can take years to sort out. There are scores of ways that your identity can be stolen. The majority of people aren't aware of just how vulnerable they are until it's too late.

How To Protect And Preserve Your Freedom, Identity And Privacy gives advice on:

- What to do if you're a victim of identity theft (a must-have just for this advice alone).
- The type of phone you should use to protect yourself from fraud.
- The tricks fraudsters use at cash machines (a real eye opener!)
- The signs to look out for which show if you have become a victim of identity fraud.
- Why you should be wary of the 'postman' knocking at your door
- How answering your phone could leave you vulnerable to fraud
- Why you should be wary about the clothes you wear

If you should be unfortunate to find yourself a victim of identity fraud then this book will tell you what you can do. For this reason alone, you need this book. It could be a lifesaver

Paperback £9.99
Published by Blue Books
Order from Publishing House • Trinity Place • Barnstaple •
Devon EX32 9HG • England
Telephone 01271 328892 • Fax 01271 328768
www.vernoncoleman.com